CENTURY
OF STYLE: LINGERIE

A CENTURY OF STYLE: LINGERIE

ICONS OF STYLE IN THE 20TH CENTURY
KAROLINE NEWMAN, KAREN W. BRESSLER
CONSULTANT: GILLIAN PROCTOR

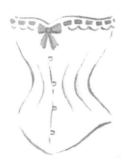

QUARTO BOOK

Published by the Apple Press
The Old Brewery
6 Blundell Street
London N7 9BH

ISBN 1-84092-077-7

This book was designed and produced by
Quarto Publishing plc
The Old Brewery
6 Blundell Street
London N7 9BH

Art Editor Elizabeth Healey
Designer Liz Brown
Assistant Art Director Penny Cobb
Picture Researchers Zoë Holtermann,
Miriam Hyman,
Henny Letailleur, Gill Metcalfe
Photographer Anna Hodgson
Illustrator Janice Nicholson
Art Director Moira Clinch

Typeset in Great Britain by Central Southern
Typesetters, Eastbourne
Manufactured in Singapore by
Eray Scan Pte Ltd
Printed in Singapore by Star Standard
Industries Pte Ltd

Contents

Part Two

Introduction

Lingerie. The very word is quintessentially feminine, filled with a sense of excitement, sensuality, and delicacy. It suggests so much more than the mundane collection of everyday underwear—panties, briefs, bras, and stockings—that a woman wears under her clothes. Although the word "lingerie" stems from the French linge, meaning linen, it has come to describe all manner of delicate, elegant, and often seductive articles of underwear made not just from linen but also from lace, silk, and chiffon, as well as man-made fibers. Although specialist items of underwear do exist—from the nursing bra to medical support tights—these items are generally too practical or functional to be included in the modern definition of "lingerie" as being sexy and fashionable.

The tie that binds: corsets (*top*) are pulled tightly for support and shape.

Slips and dips: this Janet Reger designer slip (*right*) compliments figures by clinging in all the right places.

Out of this world: this futuristic corset saves the day for Jane Fonda (*right*) in *Barbarella*.

Scarlet fever: La Perla (*below*) heats things up with a red satin bra and pants set and black chiffon tied cover.

As foundationwear, lingerie is the basis upon which a woman creates her silhouette and builds her sense of identity. These are her most intimate clothes, a personal and often secret expression of her mood worn from the bedroom to the ballroom. Her choice of lingerie will affect her behavior and set the tone for the events that follow, whether they include a busy day in the office, a work out at the gym, or a romantic dinner.

The earliest known pieces of underwear can be traced back to the ancient civilizations of Egypt and Greece, when it seems their use was purely functional. Tomb paintings show the Pharaohs wearing socks, presumably to keep the sand out of their toes, while early Minoan vases depict women athletes strapping up their breasts for support. But although a very early prototype of the bra, known as a strophium, was in use in Roman times, many of the standard undergarments worn by women today are relatively modern inventions. Panties were only introduced in the late nineteenth century, for example, as before then it was considered unhealthy for a woman to wear anything beneath her skirts except petticoats.

In the Middle Ages, members of the European nobility began to wear simple linen clothes under richly decorated and expensive outer dresses. This both protected these expensive costumes from dirty bodies, and provided a layer of warmth for the wearer; in those days homes were extremely cold, and people rarely took a bath. As clothes and fashions changed, underwear took on a new significance: it became the foundation to which outer clothes were

The sexy lineup: Can-can girls (*left*) get their kicks from lacy lingerie.

molded and shaped.

The earliest forms of the corset emerged in the fifteenth century to fulfill this role. The rigid center piece, known as the basque, was often decoratively carved and even enjoyed a vogue as a lover's token, to be worn as close to the heart as was physically possible. In addition to the corset, elaborate farthingales, hooped petticoats, and bustles created a framework, quite literally, for the robes worn as outer garments. The wide-hipped Elizabethan fashion of the sixteenth century which popularized the farthingale was designed to focus attention on a woman's childbearing hips, perhaps suggesting fertility. The fashion became greatly exaggerated during the seventeenth century when the frame achieved extraordinary proportions, used as an ostentatious display of the rich, highly decorated dress fabrics of the day.

During the nineteenth century, the quantity and style of underwear worn by women reached extremes. So inaccessible did the female body become beneath the layers of underwear that taking it off created its own form of sexual excitement and spawned the first striptease shows. The bustle emphasized women's bottoms, and frilled pantaloons and multiple layers of petticoats created full skirts. A contrast in volume between the upper and lower parts of the body was created by bodices and tightly laced corsets. Whereas the corsets of the Middle Ages were highly ornamented and worn as decorative outer clothing, the restricting corsets of the nineteenth century were strictly unseen. These mandatory garments were designed to constrain and shape the woman's body, their construction increasingly complex and their very use an analogy of female repression in Western societies. Some of the most tortuous, and dangerous, were made of steel—it is little wonder that the late nineteenth-century Rational Dress Association campaigned in favor of more natural clothing.

As the twentieth century arrived, women were controlled in every aspect of their lives, and not just by their corsets. Just a whiff of an ankle was a tantalizing sight in the 1900s, momentarily peeking out below full skirts and surrounded by pantaloons. But a revolution in the way that women thought of themselves was just around the corner, and the phenomenal changes in a woman's lingerie over the next 100 years reflected those wider concerns.

The link between lingerie, sexual politics, and female emancipation became evident as women rejected the corset both during and after World War I. Instead, the flappers of the 1920s adopted a looser, androgynous style, its ambiguous sexuality perhaps compensating for the shortage of eligible men during that decade, thanks to the enormous number of casualties during the so-called Great War. This clear evidence of lingerie reflecting women's attitudes appeared again and again through the twentieth century. The tight-waisted, fashionable New Look of 1947, which was launched at the end of World War II, was relatively shortlived; women were not prepared to wear the waist-reducing "cinchers"—modern corsets—which were required to create the essential hourglass figure. When the contraceptive pill was launched in the 1960s, the sexual freedom this gave women was mirrored in the lingerie

A delicate subject: in the 1920's, corset prints and fabrics (*above*) turn feminine and flirty.

Slip covers: this sexy satin duo (*right*) features a scoop-neck slip with a matching white wrap.

Steppping out: models strut their stuff (*left*) in a chorus line of lingerie.

Sssssseriously sexy: a matching bra and pants in a snakeskin print (*right*) by Gossard

world. Bare midriffs and the miniskirt required little or no underwear, and the layers of petticoats worn by women just 60 years earlier were reduced to matching sets of colorful and patterned bras and briefs. Gone were stockings and garters (suspenders), and in their place were the first pairs of pantyhose.

Bras went out of fashion in the 1970s—many women considered wearing bras to be "colluding with their own oppression"—but returned in the 1980s on women's own terms. Under the confident outer garments worn by office workers, typified by the broad-shouldered power suit, were flirtatious, feminine camisoles which revealed that women were approaching their sensual side with equal confidence.

As sexual interest in the various erotic zones moved around the female form, different lingerie pieces and styles went in and out of fashion. The French artist Henri de Toulouse-Lautrec caused a furore with his paintings of girls in "froufrou" petticoats dancing the decadent cancan at the Moulin Rouge in Paris in the 1890s, while stockings took on great significance when hemlines rose in the 1920s. The projectile bosoms of the 1950s, created by wearing stitched cone bras, focused on the breast before sexual interest went thigh high with the introduction of extremely short skirts in the 1960s. The bottom became the center of attention in the 1970s as leggings and jeans were molded to the body, and in response, the minimal thong arrived to take the place of more substantial panties.

Of course, lingerie can also be erotic in its own right, as well as simply highlighting an erotic zone. Perhaps this is why lingerie is one of the most popular gifts for men give to their girlfriends or wives—it is a token of intimacy. (Sadly, all too frequently he gets the size wrong. According to London's famous lingerie boutique, Janet Reger, the shop is overwhelmed by men buying glamorous pieces of underwear before Christmas and filled with women exchanging sexy bras and see-through nighties in January!)

Both the color and fabric of lingerie provide sexual signals of their own. White, traditionally associated with purity, is frequently worn by a bride as part of her wedding trousseau; black suggests sophisticated sensuality; bright red is thought raunchy, overtly sexy and faintly

A winning pair: this playing card (*left*) displays the daring designs of Agent Provocateur.

Starlet style: a provocative pink negligee (*right*) is paired with a racy black basque, suspenders and fluffy slippers.

9

Moment of triumph: French bombshell Brigitte Bardot (*right*) displays the effects of Triumph's 1953 unique cone-shaped bra.

In the knick of time: this model (*below*) shows off a white-hot set from Knickerbox.

Over exposure: A camisole is taken from the bedroom to the runway (*right*) as part of Dolce & Gabbana's outerwear collection.

immoral. As early as 1902, the English fashion writer Mrs. Eric Pritchard noted that, "the Cult of Chiffon has this in common with the Christian religion—it insists that the invisible is more important than the visible... Dainty undergarments... are not necessarily a sign of depravity." To this day, silk and chiffon are synonymous with luxury, whereas cotton and polyester are more likely to be for everyday wear. Fur adds a frisson of its very own, whether worn as mink garters by Wallis Simpson, the Duchess of Windsor, or imitated in fake fur briefs by the unconventional English designer Vivienne Westwood.

According to The Sunday Times (London) in September 1997, "Paying an exorbitant amount of money for a small exquisite thing that could so easily be lost or ruined is thrilling in its own right. Besides, let's not forget one of the purposes of underwear. It is there not only to seduce, but to enhance any seduction that might already be taking place. If a man doesn't notice your underwear, there's something wrong with him." Which begs the question, is a woman wearing lingerie for her personal sense of wellbeing, or for the potential attentions of her lover? The two reasons are often inseparable.

Although lingerie's development may be used to chart the liberation of women's lifestyles, one of its original functions—to act as "foundationwear" for stylish outer clothes—is as important today as it ever was. As Christian Dior pronounced, "Without foundations, there can be no fashion," and although women of the 1990s would find it hard to embrace the restrictive underwear of their tightly-laced, corseted, and petticoated ancestors, the revolutionary fabrics of the twentieth century provide them with just as much support, albeit in a far more comfortable fashion. Their ancestors, in turn, would hardly recognize the unrestrained, liberated bodies of today, clothed in underwear that gives both physical support and freedom of movement.

In fact, corsets have been worn beneath clothes throughout the twentieth century, whether disguised as longline bras or roll-on corsolettes. They even returned to their medieval function, employed by haute couture designers such as Norman Hartnell and Christian Lacroix as elaborate outerbodices for evening dresses. Ironically, as we enter the twenty-first century, some modern women are once more choosing to wear traditionally styled corsets to restrain their natural form, as often as not combining the corset's dual roles as an item of fashion and fetishism.

So fashionable had lingerie become by the late 1980s that many of the world's most famous clothes designers created their own selections of lingerie. In many cases, the items sport a designer label, so providing underwear with cult

Tickled pink: Made famous by Madonna herself, Jean Paul Gaultier's rose pink lycra corset (*right*) would be a stretch for anyone other than the Material Girl.

status. Gone are the discreet advertisements for ladies' underwear in women's magazines. In their place, scantily clad models appear large on billboards and buses for everyone to see. Fashion model Eva Herzigova became famous for her cleavage, amply displayed in a provocative advertising campaign for The Wonderbra with its strapline "Hello Boys," while Hollywood actresses launched their careers on the back of lingerie promotions for such companies as Frederick's of Hollywood.

In the buff: undergarments are barely-there (*left*) in new nude styles.

Modern art: as modelled in the Wolford catalogue (*below*), ordinary black sheer tights are redefined with a white stencilled applique.

The glamour of Hollywood has long been associated with women's underwear. Indeed, the film industry has been directly responsible for some of lingerie's most important innovations, right back to the days when rustling petticoats interfered with the soundtrack when "talkies" first appeared. As a result, the simple slip was introduced, worn by the Sex Goddesses of the 1930s under the fashionable sleek, figure-hugging dresses of the day. Jayne Mansfield's remarkable cleavage was featured in the 1950s film The Outlaw, supported by Howard Hughes' cantilever bra, while the pop star Madonna, famous both on and off screen, made underwear her icon. Her influence on the wardrobe of young women from the 1980s onward brought lingerie into the popular domain as a mainstream fashion item.

Many of these new lingerie styles would not have been possible without the extraordinary advances in the twentieth century of both textiles and technology. The importance of man-made fibers cannot be underestimated, affecting cost, fit, and comfort of all types of underwear. The introduction of artificial silk (art silk) during the 1920s made attractive underwear affordable for everyone; prior to this time, only wealthy aristocrats and the middle classes enjoyed decorative lingerie. Whalebone, that slightly flexible staple of the nineteenth-century corset, was replaced by vastly more comfortable elastic, while DuPont's invention of nylon in 1937 revolutionized the fit of stockings and tights, as well as petticoats, slips, and nightwear, when it went into mass production during the 1940s and 1950s.

An extension of DuPont's research led to the elastomerics, better known as Spandex and Lycra, stretchy fabrics which literally changed the shape and construction of all underwear. Three times more powerful than elastic, the phenomenal strength and lightness of these fabrics heralded the arrival of body-controlling sportswear and subtly supportive sheer tights, especially when combined with other fibers for added softness and comfort.

It is only during this century that lingerie has changed so dramatically. Sexual politics, modern technology, a rapid succession of fashion styles and the development of global communciations in all its forms—television, newspapers, and film—have conspired to blur the line between outerwear and underwear. Certainly, by the end of the 1990s, clothes designers of all sorts were increasingly influenced by lingerie styles. According to the American designer Josie Natori, "Lingerie-inspired clothing is here to stay because … it's provocative in a positive manner." It remains to be seen whether Vivienne Westwood's belief, that "fashion is eventually about being naked," is reflected in lingerie design of the twenty-first century.

1

Corsets, Basques, and Bustiers

For centuries, the female body has been molded into a variety of shapes to suit the fashions of the day, sometimes drawing attention to the bust, at other periods focusing on the bottom. The corset, in particular, has had a crucial role in achieving the desired line, at times draconian and matronly, at others comfortable, sexy, and even downright erotic. Over its long history, its distinctive form has been used both as outer and as underwear—the earliest known corset, found on a

sculpture of a Cretan snake goddess from around 2000 B.C., shows a woman wearing a laced structure to support breasts which are bare, pushed upwards, and outwards. Whereas the corset was the most private of women's garments at the start of the century, it had become flamboyant, defiant outerwear, associated with sexual fantasy and eroticism by the year 2000. Such a complete and rapid transformation of its role reflects the depth of social change and developments seen around the world in the 1900s, coupled with the effects of a revolutionary new fabric—Lycra.

A core fashion piece: the corset was the foundation of women's fashion for centuries. This version (*above*) makes a shoe look easy to tie up!

Going for gold: this award-winning color (*right*) did more than just boost a woman's attitude.

All the right curves: the S-shaped corset (*above*) featured a small waist and a seriously sexy silhouette.

TRACING THE CORSET'S LINE

The modern-day corset derived from a stiffened linen underbodice which first appeared in Europe in the 1300s. Known as a *cotte*, Old French for a close-fitting garment, it was made in two parts, front and back, with paste inserted as a thickener between two layers of linen to stiffen it. By the end of the century the *cotte* was more complex and generally known as a *basque*, although the garment changed its name frequently, from a "pair of bodys" in the 1600s to "stays," or a "pair of stays" in the 1800s. The word *corset* was introduced as a refinement.

In 1832, a Frenchman, Jean Werly, patented the first woven corset to be made on a loom, its shape an integral part of the weaving method. With the arrival of the bustle in 1870, attention was focused on the shape of women's hips and bottoms as well as waists, and a long, curvaceous figure became the aim. It was achieved with the notorious S-bend corset which actually distorted the female physique and badly affected women's health, impairing both respiration and reproduction.

In the late 1800s, objections to such extreme corsets were being voiced. In Britain, the Rational Dress Association highlighted the dangers of tight lacing, supported by the medical fraternity. But fashions of the new era, the *Belle Epoque*, required women to have a lavish bust, a tiny waist, and curvaceous hips, a shape personified by the actress Lily Langtry, mistress of Britain's King Edward VII.

As women were increasingly encouraged to participate in sports such as golf, tennis, and cycling, they chose the new "sportswoman's corset," or "health and freedom" corset, cut high over the hips for greater mobility. It had less lacing and the novelty of two attached garters (suspenders)—previously, garters were sold separately and attached to the front.

But despite the availability of a lighter, healthier corset, the emphasis on the small waist persisted, together with the elongated shape of the period. The "S-bend," or "Gibson Girl," silhouette was immortalized by the drawings of American artist Charles Dana Gibson, and popularized on the London stage by the actress Camille Clifford.

The beginning of the end

But such restriction was bound to end. In 1907, a young French couturier, Paul Poiret, created the style for modern dress with his "Neoclassical Look," and for the first time in fashion history, women could stand upright. "It was in the name of liberty that I proclaimed the fall of the corset," said Poiret in his biography *My First Fifty Years*, "and the adoption of the *brassière*, which, since then, has won the day."

Corset designers struggled to find an answer to Poiret's new fashion ideas, producing the less constricting "rational corset bodice" in 1910, but the dance craze of the early 1900s had an even more dramatic effect. Freedom of movement for dancing was vital as ragtime music and dances such as the tango, turkey trot, and bunny hug swept the whole world. As a result, the arrival of the "dancing corset" was greeted with acclaim. More like a girdle, it had side panels of zigzagged elastic, and fastened either by lacing down the back or with hooks down the side. When the American dancer Irene Castle appeared in London wearing the dancing corset, she caused an immediate stir, her lithe, acrobatic style, boyish figure, and bobbed hair the forerunners of the androgynous "flapper" look so soon to arrive.

The classic cut: women were set free from past restrictive styles, as illustrated by the original Gibson Girl (*left*), and were allowed to perfect their postures.

Bust basics: Corsets became staples in women's wardrobes, as an abundance of styles and shapes, like the Warner's Bros. Coraline (*left*) were made available to flatter different women's figures.

By 1915 Europe was at war, forcing women into munition factories, hospitals, and landwork. For the first time women were expected to take active working roles, and they demanded a corset that supplied greater physical freedom as well as support for the back. The "Jenkyns Corset," for example, incorporated the "Jenkyns Lacing Principle," a back lacing system which laced over the lower back, crossed over the hips, and buckled at the front. A deeper corset was needed, too, to prevent the practical, slimline wartime skirts from riding up over the thigh. Some stretched up to 22 inches (56 cm) down the leg.

The freedom of the flapper

In the aftermath of the war, women modeled themselves upon a boyish ideal. The cult of slimness was already well in place when Vogue magazine wrote in 1922, "with the aid of the *corsetière*, the physical culturist and the non-starchy diet, shall we soon develop a race of slender, willowy women? After all, how much more enjoyment can one get out of life if one is slim and active, and excess of *avoirdupois* leads to inactivity and boredom. Long live the mode of slimness."

Not every woman found it easy to achieve this, however. Rubber corsets worn next to the skin were advocated to "promote perspiration, as this is how reduction takes place," although a buyer at Paris's Bon Marché department store was sure that "women will never wear rubber next to the skin." The Etablissements Kretz (founders of the modern French firm, Chantelle SA) was among the first to insert elastic strips into corsets despite some scepticism about the new elasticized fabrics.

More comfortable was the *corselette*, first introduced in 1919 in America to help the fuller figure achieve a slimline look. It was a cross between a slip, a brassière, and a corset, combining a light bodice with shoulder straps and elongated, compressed side panels in loom elastic which extended from the waist to mid-thigh. When the design was introduced into Europe in the early 1920s, one French manufacturer quickly improved on the original, patenting a knitting process which created a similar garment to a shaped tube of pink silk jersey.

A surprising diversity of combined and/or separate undergarments emerged. Despite their boyish exterior, women opted for underwear that was exquisitely feminine. Light, draped, and almost ephemeral, such lingerie was often made in pinks, from rose to peach, yellow, blue gray, jade, violet, orange, scarlet, and black. Typical of the new designs was the corslo-pantaloon,

"Waspie" wonders (*right*): from high-fashion, padded versions made in heavy satin to boned, back-laced versions, the Waspie was "in"—way before it turned up in 1980's yuppie closets.

Fabrics of the early decades

By the late 1930s, a vast selection of materials were employed in lingerie, as this list reveals:

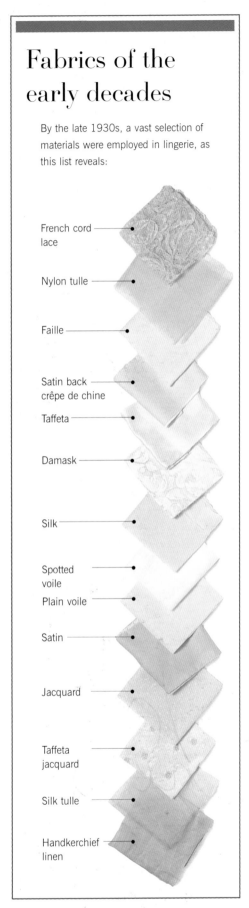

French cord lace

Nylon tulle

Faille

Satin back crêpe de chine

Taffeta

Damask

Silk

Spotted voile

Plain voile

Satin

Jacquard

Taffeta jacquard

Silk tulle

Handkerchief linen

Pretty powerful: passionate prints and flirty fabrics gave these 1920s corsets (*left*) a lighter more feminine edge.

advertised as "the equivalent of chemise, knickers, corset and camisole, and have secured the naturally supple and straight slender figure effect which is absolutely demanded by the new fashion." It was made in cotton, silk tricot, and *crêpe de chine*.

New fabrics for a new decade

Although the brassière was well-established as a separate garment by 1928, its function often overlapped that of the corset. A longline bra would restrain the rib cage, for example, while a smaller corset constrained the hips. Toward the end of the decade, the bra and smaller corset combined to create the technically advanced corselette of the 1930s, which had loom elastic that extended from waist to thigh and a side fastening of hook and eyes.

Corsets of the 1930s had largely dispensed with lacing and boning. Technological advancements in man-made fabrics had resulted in materials with two-way stretch such as Lastex, developed by the Dunlop Rubber Company in 1929. Rayon by Courtaulds in 1930 was another. Such lightweight elasticized corsets offered support and restraint without physical danger.

The slimline, smooth, and curvaceous fashions of the 1930s were increasingly dominated by the

Sucking it in: Scarlett O'Hara's *Gone with the Wind* corset (*right*) is tied as tight as possible—In *Titanic*, Rose goes through the same dress stress.

studio stars of Hollywood. As the film industry began to exert its influence upon the public's consciousness, women identified with the silver screen "sex goddesses" and wanted to copy the make-up, and the dress styles of actresses such as Greta Garbo, Marlene Dietrich, Jean Harlow, Mae West, and Joan Crawford.

The invention of the talkies had another, more indirect impact on lingerie. As rustling petticoats interfered with sound recording, alternative synthetic materials were developed to solve the problem. The resulting corselettes, Sleekies, had a smooth gloss finish and the film-going public sought them out in department stores in droves. By 1935, Lastex, described as a "wonderyarn," was being combined with other fabrics to make such hybrids as Satin Lastex, Gripknit, Controlastic, and elastic net.

Ensuring the perfect fit

Coinciding with the innovation of man-made fabrics and their application to corsetry was a new type of fastening which revolutionized both under and outerwear. In 1931, the zipper was invented in America, and by 1934–5 it had been refined into the Lightning Zip, the ideal solution to fastening corselets. But although these comfortable corsets created the sleek, glamorous contour, the manufacturers realized that professional fitting was required if women were to purchase the right size.

Leading corset manufacturers on both sides of the Atlantic, such as Warners, Gossard, and Avro, took on responsibility for professionally training qualified fitters who established a vital link between the corsetry industry and the customer in the store. Some department stores such as Marshall and Snelgrove in London even hosted special corset-fitting weeks, while Berlei introduced their official corset sizing system.

As sports gained in popularity, many of the women playing tennis, cycling, riding, and skiing wore specialist underwear such as the "sport corset" of 1934. This shorter corset which controlled the hips had a 2 inch (5 cm) elasticized waistband and was cut higher on the thigh. It was, in fact, a precursor to the girdle. The following year the British magazine *Corsetry and Underwear* announced that "the pantee corset is sweeping triumphantly into the bestseller class of leading fashion houses and is destined to make fashion history." By the 1940s this prophesy had come true, despite the onset of World War II.

Wartime influences

War in Europe had broken out in 1939, but fashionable Americans had little to worry about and wealthy Europeans did their best to ignore the chaos around them. Although the 1940s started on a glamorous note—"The only thing you must have… is a tiny waist," wrote *Vogue*, held in if necessary by super-lightweight boned and laced corsets. There isn't a silhouette in Paris that doesn't cave in at the waist"—such insouciance was shortlived.

Large-scale wartime economies soon made materials scarce and lingerie a luxury, and corsetry became utilitarian in both function and style. With more and more women working in the factories or on the land, corsetry was given a reprieve from clothes rationing because women required underwear which supported their backs during this labor-intensive period. Mary Anderson, director of The

All covered up with nowhere to go: Full-size corselettes (*above*) created sleek silhouettes. This pale pink version boasts full straps for garters.

Still sleek: This mini-mannequin (*left*) was the base for a pale pink corset with full-length skirt from Gossard.

Nouveau chic: Dior's New Look (*above*) was centered around the corset. It was a fresh foundation for any cutting-edge fashion.

Show-stopping silhouettes: Marilyn Monroe (*above left*) and Jane Russell (*above right*) in *Gentlemen Prefer Blondes*, wearing corset-inspired cuts.

Women's Bureau of the Department of Labor in the United States, declared that corsets were essential to the performance of women's war work, explaining that performance was impaired by lack of support, and that fatigue and backache were directly responsible for women leaving their war jobs. A similar complaint in Britain led the government to classify corsetry as an "Essential Works Order," ensuring that earlier standards of production and design were reinstated.

With the end of hostilities in 1945, European women once more craved glamour despite the continuing years of rationing. Christian Dior gave it to them with his New Look, launched in Paris in 1947. "No more spiv shoulders, but a tightly belted waist with full skirts over padded hips ... only in Paris could these clothes have been made; only in Paris could such a daring experiment have been undertaken" was the comment of the British *Picture Post*, which also noted, "Paris forgets this is 1947. There can be no question about the entire unsuitability of these new fashions for our present life and times ... Think of doing housework, or sitting at a typewriter all day or working in a factory, tightly corseted and encumbered and constricted with layers of hip padding and petticoats. Our mothers freed us from these in their struggle for emancipation and in our own active, workaday lives there can be no place for them."

The key to the New Look was its tiny, "cinched" waist, achieved by a new style of corset originally designed by Marcel Rochas in 1945. Known in the U.S. as the cincher, in Britain as the waspie, and in France as the *guimpe* or *guèpiére*, the corset had a boned waistband of just 5–8 inches (12–20 cm). By the following year, it had evolved on the one hand into the waistliner, incorporated into a petticoat, and on the other into a lighter, boneless garment with a built-in brassière. "A figure's not God-given," wrote *Vogue*. "Grace depends upon good exercise, good corseting. The exercise is up to willpower; the corset to wise choice."

American independence

Americans were slower to adopt the New Look, having in the intervening war years developed a strong, independent style of their own. By using scientifically developed fabrics and new manufacturing techniques such as the warp knitting machine, the introduction of two-way stretch fabric ensured that America grabbed the lion's share of the market.

Another American company, DuPont, introduced nylon, which it patented in 1937. Nylon's lightweight properties were used to create nylon taffeta, nylon marquisette, and nylon voile, which were cheaper to produce than conventional fabrics, yet offered greater freedom of movement, necessary support, and even dripped dry. More influential still was nylon elastic net, a stretchy mesh which eliminated the need for busks, lacing, and boning. Elastic net, which later became known as "power net," led to a new generation of "foundationwear" which manipulated the figure into a variety of overtly sexy shapes.

By 1954, the first corset to incorporate two-way stretch was on the market. "The Little X," launched by the American firm Silhouette, was the first of many such garments to come. Two-way stretch elastic corsets could be rolled on in much the same way as stockings, so hooks and eyes were kept to a minimum.

Hollywood continued to influence women's fashions worldwide as their latest generation of sex goddesses displayed a firmly controlled bottom, a mere hint of a stomach, and a serious bust. Marilyn Monroe in *Gentlemen Prefer Blondes* (1953) epitomized the contemporary shape, following a trend set by Lana Turner in *The Merry Widow* (1952). Turner scandalized a conservative public with her appearance in a corset, although just ten years later a similar corselette, Warners' "The Merry Widow," was on sale.

Lingerie manufacturers leapt to the assistance of less well-endowed women with plastic and rubber inserts, padding, quilting, and spiral stitching. So effective was the trend that by 1955, three out of every four British women attending the Corset Guild Convention admitted wearing falsies of some description. "Every woman who has reached the age of fashion reason knows it: her figure's as contemporary as her corsetry" declared *Vogue* in the same year.

Corsetry for couture

In Europe, many leading couture houses worked closely with the corset industry in the 1950s. The Incorporated Society of London Fashion Designers was formed to work with lingerie companies such as Berlei, while fashion houses such as Christian Dior commissioned their own lingerie designers whose models were credited at the catwalk shows. The "torsolette" was born, worn almost exclusively with evening wear, sometimes even forming the top of a couture evening gown.

These forbears of today's bustiers were the first such garments to be worn as outerwear since the Middle Ages, and the fashion quickly caught on. In Britain even the Queen's couturier, Hardy Amies, commissioned a special selection of evening "stays," which were given such exotic names as Pink Champagne and Charade. Strapless bras, basques, and bustiers were all worn wtih *décolleté* evening gowns, often incorporating tiered nylon petticoats.

Thanks to new fabric printing techniques, lingerie of the 1950s appeared in a huge choice of fashionable colors and patterns, with sapphire blue, tea rose, turquoise, coral, pinks, and peach incorporated into candy stripes and soft florals. A major proponent of printed floral nylon foundationwear was the sculptress Madame Illa Knina, who designed master patterns for the British mass-retailer Marks & Spencer.

The colors and patterns reflected the vitality of the 1950s. On both sides of the Atlantic there was social upheaval as the cult of the teenager emerged in films such as *Rebel Without a Cause* and *West Side Story*. Young women turned against the last vestiges of imposed physical restraint—their mothers were still wearing corselettes— and adopted the separate panty girdle and bra.

Once more it was the entertainment industry that had the greatest influence on corset design. This time it was the music of Elvis Presley and Bill Haley & The Comets, and the accompanying dance styles of rock'n'roll and jive. For these physically demanding dances, it was essential to move at the waist and at the hips.

In Europe, more restrained, traditionalist values were still in place, despite the fact that the aristocracy was meeting, mixing with, and even marrying fashion models, known then as *mannequins*,

Lacy looks: Fashion artist's rendition of a lacy, shapely torselette (*above*) with a wasted-away waist similar to designs which turned up in American *Vogue* in 1963.

Figure flatterer or shape sinker: When it comes to corsetry, there's no such thing as one size fits all. Choose the shape that makes you look great from Berlei's figure type indicators (*left*).

and film stars such as Grace Kelly. The stylized, urchin charm of French actress Leslie Caron and Audrey Hepburn, seen in *Sabrina Fair*, set the tone for the late 1950s.

Just before the decade ended on a pinnacle of social change, the latest in a string of great technological developments was launched. DuPont's American laboratories introduced a new fabric, "Fiber K," in 1959, which was marketed as Spandex or Elastane. Its name was later changed to Lycra, and it was to revolutionize the lingerie industry from the 1960s onward.

The impact of Lycra

"A little vanity, a little willpower—and only an ounce or two of Lycra...will make you a lighter woman," said *Vogue*. This wonder fabric was both more powerful and lighter than elastic, and was impervious to detergents, cosmetics, and perspiration. At last boning was totally unnecessary.

As a forerunner to the nude look of the late 1960s and early 1970s, Warners launched their "Birthday Suit." This revolutionary, virtually seamless garment closely resembled a swimsuit—and was made of Lycra. It weighed just 3 ounces (85 g) and cost an exorbitant amount for the times, but was a great success. Later, Warners marketed their Body Stocking along the same lines.

Lycra was a great asset in the teenage lingerie revolution of the 1960s. Companies were quick to exploit this new market which rejected all the restrictions, both physical and social, and it was Mary Quant's miniskirt which finally sounded the death knell for old-fashioned corsetry. Contemporary corsets and corselettes with their attached garters (suspenders) were replaced by tights.

Although many women over thirty remained faithful to the styles and dress code of the 1950s, the Paris fashions reflected the new mood. At the launch of her 1960 collection, the fashion designer Coco Chanel declared, "elegance in clothes means being able to move freely, to do anything with ease... those heavy dresses which won't pack into airplane luggage, ridiculous. All those boned and corseted bodices—out with them. What's the good of going back to the rigidity of the corset?"

In such a social and political climate, with women in control of their bodies for the first time since the launch of the contraceptive pill in 1963, there was no place for corsets which covered and controlled. As the department stores limited their stocks, a new phenomenon was born—that of catalog mail order lingerie companies, whose easy payment terms and traditionally styled corsets were targeted at elderly women. Even the conservative corsetry trade recognized that it had a identity problem, but it was about to receive a boost of an unexpected nature.

The origins and legacy of punk

Science fiction was all the rage at the start of the 1970s. *Barbarella* (1968) was one of many cult sci-fi films, as was *The Magic Christian*, released in 1970 and starring Raquel Welch. In it, Welch was dressed in a sculptured leather corset, suggestive, provocative, and overtly fetishistic. Before long, similar clothes were being worn by nascent punks, who emerged in London in the summer of 1976. Those with money were dressed in clothes from Sex, a King's Road

Courageous corset couture: from sci-fi cult films like *Barbarella* (above) to funky pieces that were popularized during the Eighties' punk movement.

Jean-Paul Gaultier licks the competition: his maximum impact corset (*right*) meant women no longer had to decide whether they preferred a cone or a cup.

boutique owned by designer Vivienne Westwood and her partner Malcolm McClaren which sold fetishistic and rubber wear.

Westwood used bondage as inspiration for her anarchic style. Fashioned from leather and rubber, her fetishistic corset was a cross between orthopedic support and sado-masochistic garb. It was designed as outerwear, and chimed with another London focus of the day, Richard O'Brien's stage hit *The Rocky Horror Show*. This pop musical confronted sexuality and gender stereotypes, and had its leading man dressed in corset, garter belt (suspenders), and stockings. By the end of the decade, designers from Fiorucci to Zandra Rhodes were producing punk-inspired clothing and designs for the young and even the not so young.

Westwood's influence was seen throughout the 1980s on younger designers. One was Jean-Paul Gaultier, whose costumes for pop star Madonna's "Blonde Ambition" tour of 1990 made fashion headlines. His sculptured, almost architectural corset with its conical breasts were reminiscent of the 1950s, with spiral stitching that brought breasts and cleavage into vogue once more.

Madonna was acutely aware of the impact her stage costume had on her audience of mainly prepubescent teenagers, as her performance was censored in cities such as Ottowa, in Canada, on the grounds of immorality and lewdness. But her young fans immediately adopted a diluted version of Madonna's style, wearing an array of basques and bustiers with jeans. In trend-setting department stores on both sides of the Atlantic, from Bloomingdales, Macy's, and Neiman Marcus in the U.S. to Harvey Nichols and Harrods in London, there was immediate demand for corsets, bustiers, basques, and longline brassieres. Manfacturers were quick to respond, and the look was interpreted by all the leading lingerie manufacturers, including Warners, Gossard, Charnos, La Perla, Lejaby, and Aubade.

The healthy look

Running parallel to the louche punk styles of the 1970s was a dance and health craze. The late 1970s film *Grease* summed up the disco scene, starring the actress Olivia Newton-John in a sleek, Lycra-based catsuit. Before long, dancewear showed the body in a blatantly sexual manner, with figure-clinging Lycra and Spandex leotards taking the place of underwear.

Sexpot style: a black lacy basque (*above*) gets a revealing boost from black stockings and garters.

Body-baring babes: Models wore form-fitting body stockings (*below*), down fashion catwalks to show off curves in a more comfortable form.

The age of innocence?
Cream/ivory (*right*) looks right in
not-so-subtle underpinnings.

Fashion made fun: leather leaves a
lady with everything to be desired.
The colored boa and bracelets
increase the dramatic impact of
this black base (*left*).

Lingerie manufacturers exploited this new frankness about the body, and moved from purely functional underwear to overtly seductive corsets designed exclusively for titillation. Femininity was at a premium and luxurious fabrics were commonplace, from lace, fine cotton, eyelet lace (*broderie anglaise*), matte and shiny silk and silk imitations, *crêpe de chine*, georgette, and satin to all types of Lycra, some transparent, others opaque, finished with frills, pleats, and ruching.

Two American lingerie companies, Frederick's of Hollywood and Victoria's Secrets, were renowned for their intensely feminine and sexily styled corsets, while more restrained, elegant models appeared as glamorous evening wear. These were promoted by the wedding of Britain's Prince Charles to the young Lady Diana Spencer in 1981. As a result weddings, and the accompanying wedding trousseau, were back in style all around the world, and bustiers and basques enjoyed a revival, too, creating the much-admired slim silhouette of the day.

But although a survey conducted in France in 1982 showed that 54% of women never wore elegant underwear (23% sometimes wore it and 10% often did,) attitudes were about to change. Power dressing emerged as the style for confident, professional women, and designers such as Pascale Madonna in France, Rigby & Peller in Britain, and Victoria's Secrets in America responded with a huge range of erotic, feminine underwear to be worn under the tailored suits of the day.

This fashion was epitomized by the American TV soap operas of the mid 1980s, from *Dallas* to *Dynasty*. These attracted audiences of millions around the world, mesmerized by Joan Collins (Alexis) and Linda Evans (Crystal) acting out powerful, successful, ruthless businesswomen who wore tailored, mannish suits in the boardroom and provocative basques in the bedroom.

While fitness was still desired, as illustrated by stars such as Madonna and Cher, women had realized by the late 1980s that a firm shape could be achieved with a little artifice and the help of appropriately shaped "underpinnings." The corset had effectively evolved into the bodyshaper, derived from sportswear, which featured underwiring under the breasts and elasticized control panels with popper fastenings at the crotch.

Fin de siècle fantasy

In 1990, Vivienne Westwood launched her "Portrait" collection, which went on to have enormous influence on both couture and street fashion during the following decade. Using historical costume references about garment construction, and particularly corsetry, she introduced a contemporary corset that was photographically printed with an Old Master painting by François Boucher (1703–1770) depicting a shepherd and shepherdess. It was designed as outerwear, an exaggerated reinterpretation of European rococo styles of the mid-1700s accompanied by a cage skirt and very high platform shoes.

"Not many people buy the corset and the cage…," said Westwood in defense of her critics, "but this exaggerated silhouette that I have been working on for ten years has finally had an influence." In the following years, corsets made a complete comeback to fashion, created and celebrated by the world's leading couture designers as unashamed items of outerwear. Versace, McQueen, Westwood, Lagerfeld, and Karan all placed the corset center stage while John Galliano adapted the man's fencing jacket into a tightly fitted woman's basque, and Thiery Mugler revealed his "motorcycle bustier" worn with leather hot pants in 1992.

Elle magazine, commenting on the spring catwalk collection, announced "the hourglass is back" in 1995, the year that Karl Lagerfeld invented the corset-belt. His eye-catching patent was based on the 1950s cincher, and his autumn/winter collection included a new silhouette described as "elongated *élégante*" which featured a bodyshaping slip made with a corsetlike construction. He promised it would skim two dress sizes from a woman's body, declaring "It's not a corset, it's a caress."

Keeping apace with the catwalk, ready-to-wear corsets soon appeared in fashionable department stores, and specialist lingerie shops sprung up, including Agent Provocateur in London. As the corset trade revived, corset craftsmen such as Mr. Pearl or Fakir Musafar once more emerged as the savior of women, designing for Hollywood stars, leading entertainment figures, and the couture business as they had in the 1920s and 1930s. Others, such as the Australian designer Colette Dinnigan, looked even farther back. Her strictly boned corsets and "waspies" which elongated the waist returned to the very earliest techniques employed in corset construction combined with mere wisps of lace.

The line was blurred between underwear or outerwear, and lingerie had traveled full circle. A century that began with the voluptuous, womanly silhouette contained by the S-bend finished with Versace's new "Versatile" label, especially designed for curvaceous women, the first collection to revel in such shape for decades. But as in the first years of the century, body-hugging underwear was essential to make the collection work and create the correct shape. It seemed that Christian Dior was correct when he stated, "Without foundations, there can be no fashion."

Embroidered edges: some fancy stitching adds interest to this corset shape (*above*).

Bustin' out: this artist's interpretation of the bustier (*left*), set in the *Philadelphia Museum of Art*, appears to be less comfortable to wear on the inside than it is to study from the outside.

Wacoal

The success of the first lingerie company to be set up in Japan, Wacoal, is owed at least in part to the philosophy behind the company's slogan: "Be beautiful, be beautiful, be more beautiful." Founded soon after the end of World War II, the company's ambitious fifty-year business plan has borne fruit, taking Wacoal's lingerie into upscale department stores around the world.

Understated elegance: The high-cut brief in micro-mattique polyester/Lycra (*above*) keeps you on the edge of your seat in style.

Returning as a veteran from World War II, Wacoal's founder, Koichi Tsukamoto, rejoined his family company of merchants selling textiles in Kyoto. A chance meeting with a bra pad inventor introduced him to underwear, and he was quick enough to spot its potential: Japanese women were beginning to adopt Western fashions, but their bust line needed enhancing for Western clothing. He developed his own padded bra working from images in American magazines—no one was making bras in Japan then—and by the end of 1949, his company, Wako Shoji, was selling and displaying its bras and garters in a local department store.

When Tsukamoto presented his long-term business plan to his nine employees in 1950, his goal was to make the company the world's greatest intimate apparel manufacturer before the end of the twentieth century. In 1956, on a visit to the U.S. and Europe, he wrote a memorandum: "We still have a long way to go before Japan's lingerie can be considered among the finest in the world," but before long, the company was selling its products to leading Japanese department stores such as Mitsukoshi and Takashimaya, their goods displayed in special sales areas with trained female lingerie sales consultants.

Tsukamoto invested all the company's capital in a dedicated factory in 1952, along with forty new electric sewing machines; and in the same year, Wako Shoji held the first lingerie fashion show in Japan with one restriction: "No men are allowed to enter." It was called a "reverse strip," in which models put on the new contraptions—brassières, corsets, and garters.

In 1957, the company changed its name to Wacoal, and by September 1964 it had grown so much that it was listed on the Tokyo, Kyoto, and Osaka Stock Exchanges. In the same month, Wacoal opened its own Tokyo headquarters building. Both were landmark achievements, and ensured that the Wacoal Corporation was set for growth.

Moving overseas

Tsukamoto's fifty-year plan had been divided into decades, and the third decade was to be devoted to overseas expansion. Fortunately for Wacoal, the World Expo of 1970, a global trade fair, was held in the Japanese city of Osaka, and the Wacoal-Riccar Pavilion attracted some 2.7 million visitors. As the decade progressed, Wacoal became one of the leading companies in Japan's lingerie industry, with its innovative technology and product design ranking among the world's finest.

In 1977 Wacoal expanded into North America, purchasing the well-established brand Teen Form, and its excellent reputation, in 1983. Teen Form provided access to the lucrative American market, targeting the first-bra teenage customer, while Wacoal introduced its more expensive, high-quality products to older, more sophisticated women. In 1984, Teen Form was renamed Wacoal America, and just a year later, *The New York Times* credited Wacoal with elevating the status of women's underwear in the United States from that of mere undergarment to a fashion item.

Wacoal's marketing concept was simple but brilliant: bras encorporating "European elegance," "American fit," and "Japanese technology" were sold within a fixed pricing policy of $20–$40. Wacoal introduced the personal service policy which had worked so well in Japan to fifteen major American department stores, including Macy's, Bullocks, Bloomingdale's, Saks Fifth Avenue, Nordstrom, and I Magnin, in

Brush up your style: Wacoal's lace cami bra with matching coordinated hipkini panties (*right*) in intricate white lace give a smooth, feminine look to underwear.

nine major cities from New York to Los Angeles. Within fifteen years, there were more than 1500 Wacoal outlets across the U.S., as well as operations in ten other countries, including France and south-east Asia.

In 1992, Donna Karan, the world renowned designer, made a business proposal to Wacoal, declaring: "I had a vision of what I wanted my Intimates to be. I needed the technology and expertise to make it happen. To me, Wacoal America was the best, the authority in the field." Donna Karan Intimates brought Wacoal to the attention of designer-brand enthusiasts worldwide, and under the leadership of the founder's son, Yoshikata Tsukamoto, it subsequently developed new product lines including daywear, nightwear, loungewear, and robes. All were created with the company's slogan, which had served it so well, in mind.

Rigby & Peller

Rigby & Peller, the British company famous for the quality of its made-to-measure corsetry and lingerie, was established in 1939 by Mrs B. Rigby and Mrs G. Peller. From the start, its elegant lingerie made of the most luxurious fabrics was individually fitted for a clientele which ranged from international film stars to wealthy, fashion-conscious socialites, and even royalty.

Just four years after the company was taken over by Mrs Seiden, Mrs Peller's cousin, in 1956, Rigby & Peller had been granted the Royal Warrant as Corsetière to HM Queen Elizabeth II, and soon after, to HM Queen Elizabeth, The Queen Mother.

To be granted a Royal Warrant of Appointment is an exceptional honor for any business, but when June Kenton became Rigby & Peller's proprietor in 1982, she was aware that the company's image needed revamping and revitalizing. It had an excellent, but somewhat old-fashioned, reputation; which, Kenton, with her husband Harold, was to change much.

In 1986 Rigby & Peller moved from its original premises in South Molton Street to a specially designed shop in Hans Road, adjacent to the department store Harrods, London. It was an astute move, aimed at attracting the elegant women who shopped in Knightsbridge, and her instinct was proved right. Ten years later, Rigby & Peller opened their second store in Conduit Street, London.

The company built its recent reputation on its personal service, supplying handmade bras for women of every imaginable size and shape. The old-fashioned notion of being measured and fitted for a bra was generally

One mastermind behind these creations: Mrs Kenton (*above*), owner of Rigby & Peller, teamed up with Mrs Rigby and Mrs Peller to create made-to-measure corsetry. The result was lingerie that was clearly up to par.

reinstated in the 1990s, and the experience of the saleswomen at Rigby & Peller ensured the company's success. Its range of lingerie was carefully fitted and beautifully made from silk and satin, as well as more conventional fabrics.

In 1988, the company launched its own label bras, basques, briefs, and suspenders, and expanded into Europe and America. A year later, as Rigby & Peller celebrated its fiftieth anniversary, the brand was introduced to a delighted audience in Japan. Its global ambitions did not stop there, when, in 1992, the company signed a worldwide licensing agreement for the Rigby & Peller collection to be manufactured by Eveden Ltd, and followed this in 1993 with the launch of the Diffusion Collection. But despite such growth, Rigby & Peller continued to be synonymous with personally fitted, luxurious lingerie right up into the late 1990s.

Check it out: Rigby & Peller's black and white tartan-patterned corset (*left*). With this kind of style, there's no need to read the fine print.

2

Camisoles and Petticoats

In the early 1900s, an era during which looking elegant was the norm, women spent a great deal of time and effort getting dressed each day. But choosing a dress to wear was the least of it, as women were required to don the proper foundations—including copious layers of camisoles, undershirts, vests, and petticoats—before the dress was even considered. By the end of the twentieth century, however, no such rules and regulations existed. A woman no longer spent hours getting ready, because she no longer had the time to do so: indeed one of the aims of the developments in fashion designs and lingerie over the last few decades has been to save on time spent getting dressed. The myriad versions of camisoles, vests, and petticoats had all but disappeared in the wake of the Lycra revolution. An exception was the eccentric mini-crini of the 1980s, which harked back to the full, hooped crinoline skirts of a century before. For these, the petticoat was revived, albeit in a truncated version for the 1990s.

Killer half-slip: Janet Leigh is seen (*above*) wearing a sexy, delicate feminine half-slip with lace floral trim in the film *Psycho,* 1960.

Sleek chic: Not always as streamlined as this body-hugging version (*right*), camisoles started out frilly and pristine. Marks & Spencer took the traditional top into the modern world with this sexy silhouette.

MODESTY PREVAILS

The camisole—also referred to as the chemise, corset cover, or petticoat bodice—was a favorite undergarment of the day. First introduced in the 1800s, this short bodice or vest with built-up straps was typically worn over a corset and was designed to cover the bosom, thus providing warmth and modesty. As often or not, they were worn with a petticoat under a sheer blouse, and were a necessity with the lace-trimmed dresses in white cellular cotton that were being widely worn on both sides of the Atlantic, such as those advertised by the Cellular Clothing Company at the turn of the century.

Most camisoles were waist-length, and they were often gathered and trimmed with lace or embroidery. The white nainsook of 1901, a soft, lightweight sleeveless cotton camisole with a low square neckline, was edged with *broderie anglaise* (an eyelet embroidery), for example, as well as machine-made lace and ribbon. It was fastened in the front with tiny pearl buttons and tied at the waist over a narrow hip basque (a woman's bodice that extends below the waistline). When they were worn with white cotton knee-length, ribbon-and-lace trimmed knickers, the two formed a solid lingerie base.

During those first years of the century, pink or cream wool and silk vests with lace insertions and ribbons were popular, as were the stiffened cotton camisoles with front fastening and a taped waist which appeared from around 1906. These were generally worn with open French knickers trimmed with bands, insertions, or machine-made lace. But when *The New York Times* reported that the Empire-style, one-piece dress was a universal fashion choice for fall in October of 1909, a new lingerie fad was born.

As ever, the new fashions of the day required specialized lingerie, and the combination was created in a search for newly narrowed underwear. Combinations were two pieces of lingerie combined to become one, like the chemise and drawers or the chemise and petticoat. There was also a vogue for cache-corsets, or corset covers. These camisoles and petticoat skirts or knickers were not new, but became more important under fitted clothes.

By 1910, camisoles were often tied at the waist and decorated with pleated fronts, lace insertions, embroidery, and shoulder straps of ribbon. Support for the bust was still an issue, however, and attention turned to improving the previously frilled and starched bust bodice. In 1912, the Army & Navy store catalog in Britain advertised bust bodices in white net or nainsook, some of which were boned and others worn crossed over at the back and tied in place. By 1916, bust bodices were lighter and shorter, and began to take the place of the old camisole, providing more cover for the bust under the transparent gowns of the day. They were worn by French and American women alike.

Camisole collections: As they grew in demand, these pretty undergarments quickly became a part of every woman's wardrobe. This frilly version (*left*) by Nanisoke, was one of the more conservative options.

How to make a dramatic entrance: In a lacy, white petticoat à la *Gone with the Wind*. This design (*right*) is strewn with pale, blue ribbon threaded through the fabric and tied at the front in a bow.

Camisoles for day were made of fine linen, voile, or batiste, and in silk for evening. Popular daytime silhouettes included the Empire patterns, sloped at the waist and tied with colored bows at the shoulders, while practically sleeveless evening chemises made of kilted gauze were elaborately decorated and embroidered.

The allure of the petticoat

Originally called an under-petticoat from the 1500s–1700s, petticoats had become a unmissable status symbol by the start of the 1900s. So much so, in fact, that all of the six dancers of the renowned 1904 Floradora dance troupe—known for lifting their lingerie-inspired silk skirts in Henri Meilhac's and Ludovic Halevy's 1869 comedy, *Froufrou*—reportedly married millionaires.

Such petticoats were worn over a basic hoop made of metal, known as the cupola coat or bell hoop. This framework gave skirts and dresses a dome shape or pyramid form, depending on the size and diameter of the hoops. They varied from pocket hoops, the smallest, to very large hoops which could be annoying and uncomfortable to wear.

The petticoats seen in the early 1900s led on from those worn under the long, formal dresses of the late 1800s. White cotton petticoats with deep pleats of up to 9 inches (23 cm) were worn during the day, although versions which were widened at the bottom for extra fullness were preferred for walking. Even in winter, women's petticoats were generally white, though made out of more suitable, warmer fabrics such as fancy alpaca, cashmere, or quilted silks.

For evening wear, petticoats in black silk reached as long as the dress or its train, with a flounce in the back. Near the turn of the century, flounces of embroidery or lace that reached the knees were often added, and such lace-trimmed petticoats of satin brocade or silk could be costly, taking up a large chunk of a woman's annual dress allowance. By the early 1900s, such undergarments were similar to slips but started at the waist. They could be either full or narrow, lace-trimmed or tailored, and long or short, depending on the garment which was to be worn over it.

Knitted wool petticoats were introduced around 1909 as the petticoat became progressively narrower, although the wider skirts of 1915 and 1916 brought the petticoat back into its heyday. By now, it was often yoked, worn close to the hips but widening as it fell, and as skirt hems began to rise, in part due to the impracticality of long skirts for newly working and sporty women, "a fashion for showing the edge of one's lace lavished petticoat below the hem of one's skirt" emerged, as noted in American *Vogue*.

Sitting pretty: a bright young thing shows some leg and flaunts the latest fashion (*above*) in lingerie for the roaring twenties.

ALL-IN-ONE COMBINATION

Serves—
AS BRASSIÈRE, VEST, GIRDLE, PANTY

BRASSIERE

VEST

GIRDLE

PANTY

Stylish New!

Serona
DE LUXE LINGERIE

Ⓐ
ALL-IN-ONE COMBINATION
$1.39

Combo dressing: Getting dressed was never this simple. The new combination lingerie (*left*) serves as a brassière, chemise, girdle, and panties in one.

Ⓐ
Tub Silk $2.98
Radium Silk $3.98

Ⓑ
Mercerized Jersey
Long 85¢ | *Short* 75¢

Flapper inspired chemises and camisoles (*above*) kept the rhythm of every woman's wardrobe in the early part of the twentieth century. Although a short-lived life was in store, the camisole will always be remembered and continuously gets revamped in more modern formulations.

As the 1900s progressed, there was less call for such full, decorated petticoats. The boyish, short, flapper fashions of the 1920s had little need for petticoats below, but did require a new line of lingerie. They inspired Thèodore Baer to invent the teddy, a straight-cut garment which combined a chemise with a short slip, or long vest with panties. Unlike the camisole, the teddy could be worn as a piece of clothing on its own.

From chemises to vests

Although the British society magazine *The Tatler* was still advertising camisoles in 1921, made from suede, stockinette, tricot, and satin coutil, these high-necked, button-fastening, starched bosom enhancers were already looking old-fashioned. More often worn were *chemises* (known as the lawn chemise by 1924 and the vest soon thereafter) which ended at the hip and were worn tucked inside knickers. They were often highly luxurious, made from fine Milanese silk, for example, and finished with net and hand-embroidered *appliqués*.

During the 1920s, vests became slimmer and briefer than traditional chemises and were more often knitted than woven in silk, cotton, or wool. Some had fancy tops with ribbon at the neck and armholes, an opera neck, and covered shoulders. More often, the vest was a practical, functional, but not a beautiful, garment. They were still commonly worn due to the general lack of central heating, and very early on vests made of interlock knit in blended wool and cotton by Wolsey were used to conserve body heat.

But while a really beautiful vest in wool and cotton mixture was in full fashion, it was not favored by women struggling for emancipation and sexual freedom. It was considered an unnecessary clothing item by many, including the younger generation, who despised it for its frumpish appearance and its connotations of middle age. Its bulkiness turned women's carefully contrived silhouettes into unruly shapes, and when worn over knickers, instead of providing a smooth line, the vest tended to curl up in lumpy rolls around the waist and hips. And as skirts narrowed, fashion editors advised readers to tuck their vests inside their girdles to avoid this problem.

When below-the-knee, pleated, wool skirts were introduced in New York and Paris in the mid 1920s, lingerie had to evolve yet again to keep up with the styles. By 1927, the floor-length waist petticoat, or waist coat, renamed the Princess petticoat, had all but disappeared, and before long, it became the Princess slip, a simpler, straight length of material with fitted panels from top to hem and no waistline seam.

Silk was often used for such garments, as well as for camisoles, chemises, teddies, and *peignoirs*, and in an increasingly vivid range of colors. Peach was all the rage, and lingerie could be found in all shades, from pale peach through to bright peach to dark.

Leaner lines for leaner times

As the enthusiastic ebullient era of the flapper drew to a close, women were becoming less carefree. In the U.S. in particular, the 1920s came to an abrupt close with the disastrous stock market crash of 1929. As the Depression years set in, everyday clothes grew narrow, long, and spare, as did the lingerie worn with them. As very, very few people could afford luxurious undergarments in rich fabrics, vests were widely worn for warmth and practicality. Most had round necks with short or no sleeves, and some were waisted with built-up shoulders or straps.

Camisoles also made a successful comeback in the 1930s, many made from triple ninon, a lightweight, transparent, open-weave fabric. Trimmed with delicate lace and broad-threaded satin ribbon in both muted pastel shades and white, these camisoles were designed to be worn without, or underneath, a corset, rather than as they were before—as a corset cover. More substantial camisoles were used in place of restrictive bodices, and one—the liberty bodice—fastened up the front with

Fancy panties: Slim-fitting undies in the softest wool give this panty set (*left*) a luxurious look and feel.

rubber buttons and included extra buttons for petticoats or suspenders.

Whereas the United States started the 1930s in crisis, Europe was to experience even worse disruption as it headed toward World War II. Although the British lingerie firm Marshall & Snelgrove was selling hooped petticoats for crinoline-effect skirts, as worn by the young Princess Elizabeth just before the war, austerity measures brought in soon after the conflicts started meant that such luxury was put aside. In this era of "Make Do and Mend," slips were made into waist petticoats and petticoats into camiknickers. When fabrics were scarce, parachute silk, a form of silk rayon or nylon, was used to make petticoats. There was plenty of parachute silk to go around, but it was harder to stitch than silk.

Loco over logos: This utility logo (*above*), labeled CC41, was a quality symbol during World War II on St. Michael's utility pieces.

Best investments: Camisoles and vests came in different shapes and styles (*below*) to suit every woman's fancy—the scoop-necked and waist-cinched versions to name but a few.....

A brighter future: the post-war brought about bright colors. This New Look dress (*right*) made women think the glass just might be half full again.

Peacetime prosperity

Once the war was over, the fashion for crinolines that had started with the 1939 film *Gone With the Wind* was refueled, at least in the U.S. Pierre Balmain designed a dress in white chiffon with black polka dots and hip swathing knotted in a soft bustle, which was shown over a pale pink tulle crinoline.

Crinolines were not worn on their own, however, and combinations of all types came into their own. There were camiknickers (combined camisole and knickers), the Corslo pantaloon (a chemise, knickers, corset, and camisole), pettivests (a petticoat and vest), and camishorts (step-in panties with a brassière for evening or chemise for day). To secure the new fashion's naturally slender figure, these pieces were often made from fine fabrics such as cotton tricot, crêpe de chine, and silk tricot.

By the 1940s, the new generation of man-made fabrics were regularly used in lingerie, and the result was a choice of stylish summer and sportswear underwear made from rayon that was affordable by far more of the population. The wealthy stuck to pure silk. But in the winter, retaining warmth was still a priority in these days before efficient heating, and winter garments were cut from wool, camel's hair, cashmere, alpaca, and llama. Flannel crinolines were worn under petticoats which were knitted, crocheted, or quilted, and stuffed with down.

Dressier versions of the crinoline turned up with pleated ruffles, alpaca, satin, or silk trims, and they were often lined with wool. But most women invested in the utility version, which was straight and pleatless, and fell just below the knee. As these were made of less material, they cost less for manufacturers to make and so were cheaper to buy, an important consideration while such petticoats were an essential part of Christian Dior's New Look, launched in Paris in 1947.

Layers of stiffened net and frills with a nipped-in waist were required for evening or partywear, the desired New Look achieved with removable hoops. Sheath skirts, another popular fashion of the decade, called for quite different styles of petticoat or slip. These were narrow, with limited trimmings to avoid creating any bulk. Petticoat frills were strategically placed to prevent stimulating thoughts of desire should they accidentally be glimpsed by an onlooker.

From New Look to new era

In the 1950s, as the world settled into a longer peace, American affluence filtered down to its younger generation. As rock'n'roll started to grow in popularity, the first teenagers set their own styles in clothes as well as music. The Froufrou petticoat was a teenage sensation, slipped on over layers of crinolines

Get shorty: An ivory cami dress (*right*) aims to show off the legs of the wearer. The close-up (*below*) shows details of floral-patterned stitching

Decorative around the edges, sheer and simple in between... these slimming French-style gowns (*right*) make under-dressing almost as fun as over-dressing.

FRENCH STYLE SILK CREPE
$1⁶⁹

K FINE KNIT RAYON PRINCESS GOWN $1³⁹

L FRENCH STYLE SILK CREPE $2⁰⁰ POSTPAID

M FRENCH STYLE SILK CREPE Two Qualities $2⁰⁰ POSTPAID and $1⁴⁹

The lingerie chorus line: Undergarments ran the gamet from strapless bras worn with petticoats to camisoles, chemises, and slips (*above*). But all of these stylish pieces boasted model status.

for dancing to the latest sounds. Every girl wanted to look like Brigitte Bardot, the buxom movie star, and dressed like the musical all-girl group The Cherelles in their wide hoop skirts.

Couture designer Pierre Balmain was a leader in the petticoat revolution, although few women could afford his exquisite designs. Determined nonetheless to show off their shapes in as full a skirt as possible, women padded out their hips with foam rubber and embellished them with ruffles, and "paper nylon" petticoats pushed out skirts for parties and dances. The Schiaparelli petticoat, designed in 1950 by Helen Hunt Bencker Hoie, was another big seller; it had a sheer circular half-slip banded with lace and was meant to be worn under big skirts.

But at the same time that the *froufrou* skirt was hugely popular with the younger set, designers such as Norman Norell were presenting their straight, seamless chemise dresses in 1950 for more sophisticated women. This slender line continued with narrow dresses nipped at the waist with flared Spencer jackets in 1951, skinny sequinned or mermaid dresses in 1952, and Empire-waist evening dresses in 1955. Most of these styles were worn with straight slips, although full-skirted petticoats did survive until 1957. Thereafter, slim skirts and sheath dresses became all the rage for the fashion-conscious, and straight slips were practically a requirement.

Straight petticoats with slits at the center front, back or side were also worn, like the espresso slip, which was straight with ruffles at the hem. Such simple lines were a preview of what was to come, as London set the tone in the 1960s with its street style.

'Honeydew' the new collection theme by Debrette

Our representatives have full details. Gordonia Debrette Limited Stoney Street, Nottingham Telephone (0602) 51148

DEBRETTE

BRI NYLON

Pretty in prints: These racy garments (*above*) turned up in different cuts. Girls could choose the shape they preferred and feel comfortable in them.

Petticoat progress: St. Michael takes petticoats to the next level by producing them in nylon reminiscent of 1950s rubber diapers (*above*). The color softens the cutting-edge concept.

Perfect for lounging: Mary Quant gave fashion an edge with sweater-shaped tops and briefs (*above*) in deep shades, bright stripes—ideal for slipping on under jeans, these pieces were favored by the young generation in the 1960s and 1970s.

The Sexy Touch: thin straps, a low neckline and the see-through fabric (*right*) offers a glimpse to more personal underlayers.

The Erosion of Underwear

The unending stream of new fabrics and man-made fibers that had appeared over the previous three decades had a radical effect on the lingerie market. Elastic in all its forms had revolutionized underwear, including the slip. Soon after elasticized waists were added to the waist slip, it was shortened to accommodate the miniskirts and dresses of the late 1960s, and then lengthened again to a wide bell shape for the knee-length skirts of the 1970s.

The 1970s, a confusing decade as regards fashion, brought about a revival of romanticism as

Back in Black: lingerie gets an edge when cut in an ebony shade. Mary Quant (*left*) gives lingerie a dose of biker chic with a strappy top and matching shorts.

All Decked Out: designer Janet Reger turns out an elaborately decorated combination (*left*) in a racy, lacy design.

women dressed up in soft, lace-trimmed camisoles and frilly petticoats that owed more to the start of the 1900s than the 1970s. As denim became truly timeless and extremely functional, lingerie started to follow suit, abandoning delicate, lacy teddies in favor of skintight Lycra bodies.

The fashion message of the 1980s was even more unclear. On the one hand, actress and pop star Madonna broke the taboo on showing lingerie in public when she dressed herself in bras, corsets, and slips to perform. This wearing of underwear as outerwear was typical of the decade, in which just about every style of lingerie since the crinoline resurfaced. Women opted for a wardrobe of luxury and abundance, embracing bustles, petticoats, turn-of-the-century camisoles, and 1950s bustiers in just a handful of these famed revivals.

Madonna's daringly sexual style made its way into mainstream fashions as silk camisoles were worn under power suits, and were paired with slinky skirts as evening tops. Vests came back in the form of embroidered long camisoles, now in tailored, woven fabrics rather than knitted, and short slips in elegantly wrapped styles were in abundance.

Audacious designers such as Katherine Hamnett and a bevy of talented Japanese designers created severely graphic clothes for broad-shouldered businesswomen. Rei Kawakubo, Japanese founder of Comme des Garçons, introduced a fetishistic edge to clothing by concentrating on abstract texture and color. Designers like Martin Margiela and Anne Demeulemeister designed clothes as art for different types of lifestyles, while Christian Lacroix cashed in on the retro age, telling *Vogue* in 1988 that "every one of my dresses possesses a detail that can be connected with something historic, something from a past culture. We don't invent anything."

With such a wide range of clothes on show, and such a nostalgic yearning for bygone times, lingerie was bound to come back into style. It played a major role in John Galliano's romantic collection, which represented the empire of dandyism, while Vivienne Westwood thrived on the pop culture of the day. Her mini-crini, created in 1985, was a perfect example of underwear turned outerwear, and before long, lace-trimmed petticoats in ivory or shell pink turned up as skirts from her designer cohorts.

The lingerie resurgence continued into the 1990s as women lived through a return to fashions of the past. Designers sent models down the catwalk in slip dresses, and actresses such as Courtney Love paraded about town in torn camisoles and slips. The singer Tori Amos wore a slip dress on an album cover, while the "Girl Power" pop phenomenon of the late 1990s, the Spice Girls, performed their songs in clothes that owed more to lingerie than outerwear.

The diversity of underwear in the 1990s was enormous. While the staid British retailer of sensible undies, Marks & Spencer, was producing waist petticoats in several lengths from nylon and polyester, the American mail order company Victoria's Secret filled the pages of their catalog with lacy, silky, and sheer versions of teddies, vests, and countless other items of exotic, erotic underwear in innovative colors and prints. The century had started with a clear understanding of what underwear was, and how it was to be worn, but it finished with far more freedom for women to choose their lingerie according to their tastes.

Stepping out in style: The vest and briefs get dressed up in lace for day or night (*right*). Smooth fabric at the center gives a streamlined effect, but the matching lace lets a girl walk on the wild side.

The perfect fit: Exquisite details add shape and interest to this body-hugging piece (*left*). Molded cups smooth the bustline, and woven lace guarantees a perfect fit and maximum comfort.

Hanro

In 1884, Messrs. Hansdchin and Ronus set up their company, Hanro, to produce luxury knitted underwear with a guarantee of quality, fit, and performance. Today, the Swiss company manufactures its garments in Switzerland, Austria, and Ireland, and sells them in more than twenty countries worldwide, including the United States, Italy, France, Great Britain, Japan, Hong Kong, and all over the Middle East.

The key to the company's phenomenal success lies in the exquisite styling of its lingerie, which puts a pragmatic combination of fashion and practicality at the heart of its four key collections: The Classic Collection, Trend Collection, and Sleepwear Collection for women, and the Classic Collection for men. The garments are made from fabrics of superb quality, and the company is renowned for choosing the finest natural materials available, from pima cotton or Egyptian cotton to Merino wool and cashmere.

More often than not, the fabrics are dyed in equally natural colors, such as white, black, and ivory. But despite its affinity with natural fabrics, the company has also experimented with the best-quality synthetic fibers on the market, incorporating new man-made materials such as microfiber and Tactel into its Trend Collection. Its "Soft Feeling" range used 80% polyamide and 20% elastan, for example, combining the smoothness of silk with a durable practical fabric that was easy to look after.

Hanro lingerie is also renowned for its smooth lines, which is achieved by making garments such as cotton camisoles and briefs with a circular technique that eliminates side and back seams. Although its selection extends from the everyday camisoles, and panties, to underwired bras and bodies, different shaped briefs, and G-strings, all Hanro's garments can be recognized by their signature streamlining.

The enduring popularity of Hanro's designs is a testament to the company's ability to anticipate and meet the trends of a market which has changed beyond recognition over the last century. In recent years, Hanro has established itself as a major manufacturer by marketing its collections through some of the world's most famous department stores, from Harrods (London) and Bergdorf Goodman (New York) to Galeries Lafayette (Paris). The upscale customers of such stores have clearly appreciated the inherent purity of style found in Hanro's lingerie.

Damart

Think of thermal underwear, and most people will immediately think of Damart. The name conjures up the idea of warm and comfortable garments for both men and women, and indeed, many famous explorers (including Sir Ranulph Fiennes) have withstood exceptionally cold temperatures thanks to Damart's exceptional underwear.

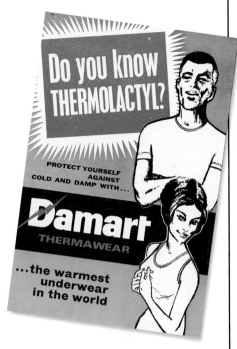

Its famous selection of thermal vests, panties, bras, and nightwear (as well as insulated clothing) is manufactured in Roubaix in France and the British town of Bolton in West Yorkshire, a town famous for its weaving tradition.

Damart owes its success to the weaving experiments of the Despature brothers who, in France in the early 1950s, noticed the remarkable insulation and water-repellent properties of man-made chlorofiber and recognized its potential for underwear. What was more, their "Thermolactyl," the result of stringent testing and development, could be knitted with fibers such as silk and wool to create perfect fabric combinations. Legend has it that the brothers discussed the breakthrough at a meeting in a café opposite the rue Dammartine in Paris—hence the name Damart.

Damart Thermolactyl underwear is extremely functional. The natural elasticity inherent in Thermolactyl provides a body-hugging fit, while its unique fibers trap warm air close to the body, simultaneously letting perspiration rise to the surface of the garment, leaving the skin dry and comfortable. The fibers can be worked into fabrics with four grades of warmth, from Thermal Light 2 through Thermal Classic 3, Thermal Plus 4, and Double Force 5,

an adaptability which has meant that Damart garments with a high Thermolactyl content can be both warm and fashionable. They are also machine washable and quick drying.

Although Damart was originally associated with purely practical underwear, its move toward attracting a new generation of Damart fans led to the creation of a range of pretty, stylish "Fancy Knits," including a delicately patterned cable knit, stretch rib knit, and

Bundle up all you want: If you're not wearing Thermolactyl, Damart's signature fabric (*above*), you might catch a cold. Here, the company's favored fiber makes its debut.

Keep warm on a cold winter's night: Slip on Damart thermal wear (*left*) under any piece of clothing—if the color doesn't warm you up, the fabric surely will.

lace-trimmed petal knit. These were so successful that by the late 1990s, Damart had more than ten million customers worldwide, with offices in Australia, the United States, Japan, and Europe, its Thermolactyl fiber renowned for its soft warmth and luxurious feel.

Chantal Thomass

With hindsight it is difficult to imagine the radical effect that Chantal Thomass' lingerie had on French women of the 1970s. When she launched her first collection of soft, feminine, and sexy designs in 1975, a time when feminism was becoming established in Europe, it was almost subversive to suggest that women's lingerie could celebrate femininity.

In 1970, the French designer Chantal Thomass designed her first collection of ready-to-wear clothes, a collection which brought her recognition as a stylish creator of fashionable outerwear. Her first lingerie pieces were conceived as accessories for her outerwear designs; made from luxurious fabrics such as silk and lace, and in colors which matched the clothes worn on top as outerwear.

These proved so successful that from 1975 to 1980, Thomass designed exclusive lingerie collections for both winter and summer seasons, which were sold through her Paris shop on rue St Sulpice. Every stylish French woman yearned to wear lingerie designed by Thomass, and clients such as the French actress Catherine Deneuve and the American actress/singer Cher were among the shop's fashionable following.

Thomass' philosophy that "lingerie is something that you wear close to your

Petal pusher: This sleek black bra (*left*) by Chantal Thomass with a subtle floral pattern gives busts a boost in style.

skin and it is the first thing that a women thinks of as she gets dressed in the morning, so her choice of lingerie will determine and affect her mood for the rest of the day. Her choice of lingerie will determine the way she walks, sits, and moves all day long. I design lingerie to make women feel good; which is simple and comfortable," proved to be an absolute winner. With accessories in mind, Chantal Thomass launched her own brand of tights in 1979—many made with lacy decoration on them. These too were an immediate success, and were stocked by top-quality department stores such as London's Harrods and France's Galèries Lafayette.

By 1980 Chantal Thomass had licensing agreements with Barbara and Wacoal, marketing and distributing her luxurious designs throughout Europe and the Far East. As the business grew, Thomass joined forces with a Japanese partner, World, but by 1996 the company had closed down.

"I gave to sexy lingerie a sense of classicism," Thomass claimed. "As a result of my approach to feminine underwear it became not only acceptable to buy beautiful lingerie, but it became chic for everybody and anybody to wear it."

Female-formed figures: This cross-stitched bag (*above*) takes the shape of a woman in a velvety fabric and straps that buckle brilliantly.

Botanical beauty: Stockings (*left*) get decked with a fresh floral motif.

3

The Brassière

Throughout the century, the brassière, a most essential piece of lingerie, has been known variously as the bandeau, the bust extender, the bust shaper, and the bust bodice. In France it is known as the *soutien-gorge*, a harness, but even the ancient Greeks and Romans had their own names for the brassière: the *mastatedon*, *mamillare* or *strophium*. The term brassière, or its informal shortening, the bra, was first introduced in the 1920s.

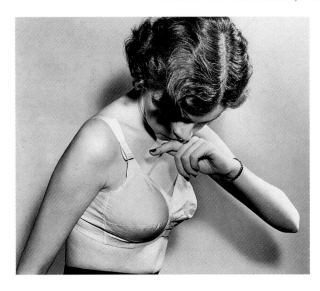

The inflatable bra: An uplifting concept: For those who have less to show or others who want what they have to show more, the inflatable bra (*above*) was born.

Animal instincts: Women could take a walk on the wild side in this leopard printed bra and pantie set (*right*). Inspired by sex kitten Marilyn Monroe, this line is cut full with a thick black trim, showing off more fabric.

During the nineteenth century, the emphasis had always been on accentuating the shape of the bottom, as seen, for example, in the S-Bend Corset, but there was a shift towards emphasising the bust instead during the course of the twentieth century. Just as its name changed through the decades, so too did the purposes of the garment. Brassières lifted, enlarged, supported, confined, flattened, revealed, and modestly covered women's breasts throughout the decades, making them the most important element in a Western woman's wardrobe. As the years passed, the bra became one of the most complex pieces of lingerie ever created, and by the late 1990s, it was composed of up to 43 components, designed with a structure and function comparable to those of a cantilever staircase or a suspension bridge.

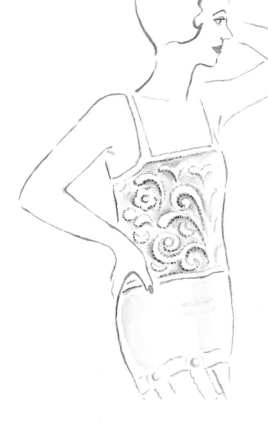

SUPPORT FOR THE TANGO

Bust improvers were first introduced into fashion in the early 1900s, although there are earlier references to impractical pre-bra garments that would make any modern woman glad to have missed them. One of the most unusual was the Lemon Cup Bust Improver, a bralike device that featured a light, coiled spring in each cup and padding made of bleached horsehair.

Although early designers had the right idea, it still took a while before a practical solution to breast support was found. In 1904, they dreamt up the cotton bust-improver, lightly boned and stitched, with adjacent shoulder straps, satin ribbon, and trimming. Next, they attempted to turn the corset into a bra by creating the corset waist, a garment closer to a corset cover or camisole made of cotton, linen, lace, and ribbon. Although it was based on the camisole until 1914, it boasted more structure, tightness, and opacity, and was typically worn for decency and comfort.

As the popularity of the corset waned, especially among those who were taken with the new tango dance craze, a new type of woven elastic material was used to create the American slip-on in 1913, a garment which offered support for those who did not opt to wear the dance corset. One young woman who disdained the corset was the American debutante Mary Phelps Jacobs (who later changed her name to Caresse Crosby). In 1914, Crosby used two hankies, a piece of baby ribbon, and help from her maid to create the first boneless, midriff-free bra.

For everday wear, lingerie dresses—lightweight, easy-to-care-for, day dresses still in style after the turn of the century—became increasingly decorative, and lingerie followed suit. Insets of lace, tucks, white-on-white embroidery, and ruffles started appearing on the new brassières, resulting in more and more ornate models. In France, the *soutien gorge*, created by Paul Poiret graduated from its simple shape with front lacing or buttons to a lacy ruffled style made from cambric with net insertions, cotton tricotrine, silk, and satin. Shape molds were added to increase the size of the bust, but offered no support to the breasts. The lightest of brassières was that created by Earrieros in 1920 in tulle and ruched pink ribbon.

These frivolous details made women more aware of their femininity and urged them to pay more attention to their own individual beauty. By the 1920s, most women would not have left home without wearing a bra. The soft brassière first appeared as a bosom flattener (constructed from a broad band of satin ribbon), but had grown less restrictive by 1925, allowing for natural curves to show through. Narrow ribbon straps, which looked dainty and insubstantial, were replaced with heavier fabrics.

The first sign of shape

With brassières becoming such a popular clothing item, more and more women found it difficult to find the bust cup that suited their size and shape. To remedy the situation, Mrs. Rosalind Klin, the Polish-born director of the Kestos Company, created the Kestos bra by folding two handkerchiefs crosswise. She joined them into one piece with an overlap in front, and added shoulder straps sewn to the points at each side of the breasts and on the end of the fabric triangles. Elastic was crossed at the back and buttoned to the brassière under each cup, which had darts under the bust for more shape. The Kestos bra became so well known that women on a shopping spree set out to buy not a bra, but a Kestos.

As the decade progressed, shape became a definite priority. Disk construction on the two sides, introduced in 1928 but not popularized until 1950, led to deeper bust cups and provided a rounded shape. The bandeau bra, made of silk elastic or tricot with two rounded cups, was designed for a figure

Can I have a Kestos please? The Kestos bra (*above*) was based on the principle of two triangles being neatly stitched together to form a comfortable bra that almost any woman could wear.

Learning how to spell did more than help a girl's vocabulary; it helped her choose her bra size. These styles (*left*) by Warner's featured the newly developed ABC cup size system that would provide women with more complete coverage for their individual bodies and shapes.

requiring an elastic hip belt and some bust control above the waist. Suddenly, the bust-designing garment took control of the undergarment world, giving new shape and style to women everywhere.

By the 1930s, the primary goal of the bra was to separate the breasts. Shaped cups, introduced with the popular triangular Kestos style, allowed the bra to support and enhance breasts of all shapes and sizes. Manufacturers added bone and produced bras with different cup sizes; padding was a priority in many of the newer versions.

As fashion of all kinds became synonymous with an expression of freedom, innovations in the design of the bra allowed women to choose how they, and others, saw themselves. Cup busts, defined busts, uplifted busts, and even accentuated busts began to fill a new fashion niche, and in 1935, Warner, introduced cup fittings for the first time. At last, someone had realized that the measurement of the bust and the size of the breasts (A, B, C, D) needed two different scales.

In the 1930s, fashions became ever more tubular as hemlines fell to the lower calf for day and the floor for evening, and the bust, waist, and hips reappeared. Evening gowns turned up either draped and body-slimming as inspired by Paris couturier Madeleine Vionnet, or in intricately draped silk jersey as produced by another Paris couturier Alix (Madame Grès.) In part, this increased acceptance of body-molding silhouettes was due to a series of advertisements for sanitary napkins, which were developed after World War I, and which emphasized wearing them under clinging fashions.

Many of these slim gowns and dresses boasted halter or bare-backed bodice cuts, as did a number of summer dresses, leading to the creation of the first strapless bra in 1934. By the late 1930s, when suits were all the rage, constructed with tailored jackets shaped to the body, bras were in demand to mold the bustline into a complementary shape. The bust, first emphasized by the clothes of World War I, was now dressed in an increasingly well-cut bra, carefully seamed for different figure types. Boned or underwired bras were worn to give breasts a more substantial silhouette.

Femininity was at an all-time high, and designers turned out hundreds of variations of the bra. There were satin, lace, net, and batiste versions, some with stitched satin undercups, others with decorative hems, and yet more with seaming on satin chiffon, rayon, and *crêpe*, with side fastenings or suspenders. Feminine shades such as pink, peach, tea rose, and apricot turned up on all types of lingerie, although most women also invested in a few bras in white. Black, however, was reserved for the luxury class only.

In 1937, the DuPont company invented nylon, a revolutionary material that was strong, light, supple, and could be woven or knitted by machine. Nylon was the ideal fabric for the construction of the bra because it was easily washable, would drip dry, and no ironing was necessary. However, nylon did not become available to the general public until the year 1938, and its full effects on bra production were not to be seen until the late 1940s.

Spirit lifters

The outbreak of World War II in Europe in 1939 drastically affected the clothing industry, from haute couture to lingerie. In one issue of *Vogue*, an advertisement for "a strapless plunged brassière top welded to alternating panels of nylon and fine elastic, strategically boned with back fastening," seemed

The power of stitching

A number of distinctive bras were launched on the market in the 1950s, including Triumph's 1953 circular-stitched, cone-shaped bra which was promoted by the French actress Brigitte Bardot. Jayne Mansfield and Marilyn Monroe also influenced the appearance of women's busts by sporting Spirella-style bras. Pointed and exaggerated bustlines of this type originated in the late 1920s and 1930s, but were popularized in the 1950s, thanks to circular stitching and stiffening inserted into the cup points.

Bridget Bardot—1958

more suited to the sale of a piece of machinery than a description of a garment. With military uniforms, and their civilian imitations seen everywhere, legs became more noticeable, and breasts became objects of irresistible desire. Mouths featured the red badge of courage, brightly painted on in beet juice. At one point, factory girls protested that they could not win the war without the help of brassières, nylons and lipstick.

As a large bust grew ever more fashionable, Hollywood made the most of a bevy of big-busted leading women to draw in both male and female audiences. Victorian-style underwear was often spotted in these pictures, and in some, the directors went too far for their times. In one famous Western, *The Outlaw* produced in 1943, the metallic bra designed for, and worn by, the actress Jane Russell inspired a legal battle to ban the film, a struggle that succeeded in keeping the film off the screens for six years.

Toward the end of the war, as lingerie of all types began to be simplified, it was a bra's durability that counted. Extravagant features and decorative edges were unaffordable, and they were left out. But once the war was over, bra designers exploited their new-found freedom, and took the bra in a completely new direction.

As more women took up tennis, riding, and skiing, bras became increasingly flexible. Bra backs and straps were completely elasticized, and sizings were improved as all bra manufacturers began to acknowledge both chest measurements as well as breast size. In 1948, the famous lingerie manufacturer Frederick's of Hollywood introduced the Rising Star, the world's first push-up bra, after designing the first padded bra the year before. The crisscross stitching on the bra cup gave it a unique uplift, and after a decade packed with hard times, the bosom was finally back.

A stitch in time: Circular stitching made the new bras all the rage (*right*). Women began busting out, thanks to innovative sewing techniques that made breasts more pronounced and often cone-shaped.

The fulsome Fifties

While it took some time for sex symbol Jane Russell to wear a racy bra in public—following the banning of the film *The Outlaw* in 1943—it was well worth the wait. In order to solve a costume problem for the film, finally being released in the early 1950s, structural engineer Howard Hughes created a wired brassière (based on cantilever engineering) with exaggerated uplift especially for her, and a generation of cleavage icons was born. Marilyn Monroe, Elizabeth Taylor, Jayne Mansfield, Brigitte Bardot, and Baby Doll Carol Baker were a generation of well-built stars who drew the attention of both male and female fans, promoting the appeal of the bra by so doing.

Bosoms were in, and both the French and Americans tried to determine which shape was most fashionable. The French aimed for the apple shape, wearing bras softly padded with foam rubber, while Americans opted for a missile look, constructing and reinforcing conelike bust cups whose pointed tips were evident through the tight sweaters then in vogue. A new fundamental fashion featuring a fluid line gave off the illusion of a woman's individual curves.

Underdressed and undecided: While lingerie didn't always get a display this public (*left*), sheer fabrics and carefully molded shapes were elegant enough to wear under any evening attire.

What's less is more: Frederick's of Hollywood gets daring with demi-bras (*left*) that expose more than necessary. Popular among women and loved almost as much by their significant others, these sexy styles made lingerie history in the 1990s.

Sixties freedom was often hinted at with the term "flower power." A company by the same name shows its fashion power with a bra (*right*) in a fresh, floral theme.

But her natural shape was not yet of interest, and women still depended on a little help from designers to achieve their desired looks.

Fortunately, by this time, the latest technology was producing a plethora of comfortable, lightweight, man-made fibers that could smooth and control the body with light elastic lingerie. The 1950s saw bras made from a variety of elasticized fabrics, from silk and cotton shantung, net satin, brocade, nylon, and power net to taffeta, satins, chiffon, and mesh.

Within a few years, lingerie companies were marketing bras with foam rubber and plastic insets, padding, spiral stitching, and other clever shaping tools to increase bust size and raise and separate the breasts. Stitching was a serious business and gave the brassiere the shape it needed to show off the form-fitting sweaters of that time.

The lingerie company Berlei introduced the Hollywood Maxwell bra, the original whirlpool brassière which had become a favorite of film stars. Available in pink, white, or black nylon, cotton batiste, and net, the whirlpool bra was finished with continuous stitching, giving perfectly rounded contours for separation and the newest forward look. These intricately shaped bras were the ideal foundations for the sweater era, which peaked in 1957. Cashmere sweaters and sweater sets were worn as tight-fitting daywear and with plunging necklines by night.

Frederick's of Hollywood, still soaring on its padded bra success, introduced demi-bras, or half-bras, that exposed the upper breasts, as well as cookies, or removable pads, which were inserted or removed from the padded bra silhouette. Front closures, usually in the form of the hook and eye, made getting dressed easier, and underwire support provided even more of a lift. And finally, there was an answer for women who had enough natural padding, uplifting, and enlarging: Minimizer bras were developed to reduce breast size by one cup size.

As actress Jayne Mansfield touted her impressive 42 DD figure well into the 1960s, bra manufacturers began focusing their undivided attention on enhancing the bust. Wonderbra, a major padded bra manufacturer, even incorporated underwire support and padding in their swimsuit designs to ensure a full, voluptuous figure for all. The bra also turned up in a variety of other forms. A brief bra and slip, known as the costume slip, which had been created by Maidenform in 1932, made fashion history in the late 1960s.

A changing order

Women of all ages benefited from the newly developed bras. The growing number of affluent teenagers in the United States provided a new market for the lingerie manufacturers, and in 1956, the first exclusively teenage lingerie fashions featured training bras—soft cupless, wireless versions specifically designed for over-eager preteens. Manufacturers also branched out into improving strapless bras for an

Mysteriously sleek: The new stretch Lycra (*above*) covered every curve and bulge, solving even the bustiest babes bra dilemmas.

Measuring up

Most women do not realize how important it is to wear a bra of the correct size, both for style and health, because the shape of the bosom changes as does the bra—both from different types of wear and tear. As a result many women are wearing ill-fitting bras. It is possible to get measured by a professional bra fitter, found in most department stores. The fitter will take two measurements: the bra size and cup size. The bra size is the measurement of the ribcage under the breast, whilst the cup size, ranging from A through to H, is the volume of the breast. To measure the cup size the fitter will measure around the fullest part of the breast. A well-fitting bra sits around the ribcage, directly under the breastline, and is neither loose nor riding up at the back. The central panel of the bra separating the cups should sit flat against the breastbone. A badly fitting bra cuts into the back, and with small cups, the breast will "overflow". Different bra styles will create different effects; the Balconette lifts the bosom forwards; and the classic bra provides a smooth outline. There is no international standard for bra sizes, but a rough guide is: US, UK: 30, 32, 34, 36, 38, 40, 42 44 (in); Australia: 10, 12, 14, 16 (based on clothes' sizes); and Europe: 70, 75, 80, 85, 90 (cm).

Six degrees of alimentation: Offering bust support for six different types of dresses, this eclectic bra (*right*) adapts to a halter back, low sides, criss cross, low back, and stretch strap version.

even sleeker silhouette under the halter neck and backless evening dresses that were all the rage. Some evening and cocktail dresses contained built-in brassières to relieve the wearer of putting on an additional undergarment.

Nonetheless, the bra began to lose its importance as a fashion item, although it also gained status as a political statement. During this era of individual expressionism, seen in events such as the 1960s pop festival Woodstock, political rallies, and peace movements, semi-nudity or nudity was in the spotlight. As clothes skimmed the body, women no longer needed underwear that imposed on them, and many thought of the bra as the symbol of the oppression of femininity.

But while daring women went without them, most wore a lightweight version like Rudi Gernriech's "no-bra bra." In 1964, Gernreich introduced this bra without the intention of its molding the breasts in specific shapes, but in an attempt to cover them comfortably. Some women favored light-as-air stretch bras, bikini underwear, and the occasional half slip. Those who did not discard their bras but still believed in what the act symbolized simply cut out the nipples, so they could at least say they tried to make a point.

In 1965, Gernreich grew even more creative and launched his Exquisite Form collection of sheer tricot nylon in white, black or, the most popular, nude. The hippie generation, which dressed in tie-dyed and flower-power motifs, inspired the same designs to appear on bras and panties. In 1968, Emmanuelle Khan designed a white tulle bra with strategically placed white lace flowers for Erys, and in 1969 Ungaro flirted with the technological silhouettes of the future and designed metal bras.

This vogue for transparent fashions was taken to extremes by designer Paco Rabanne's plastic minidress of 1965, made of linked plastic and metal disks. But those who chose not to leave all on display found creative bra styles to wear and innovative ways to wear them. Some opted for bras done up in animal prints, spots, and splashes of color, many of which were sold with matching panties, slips,

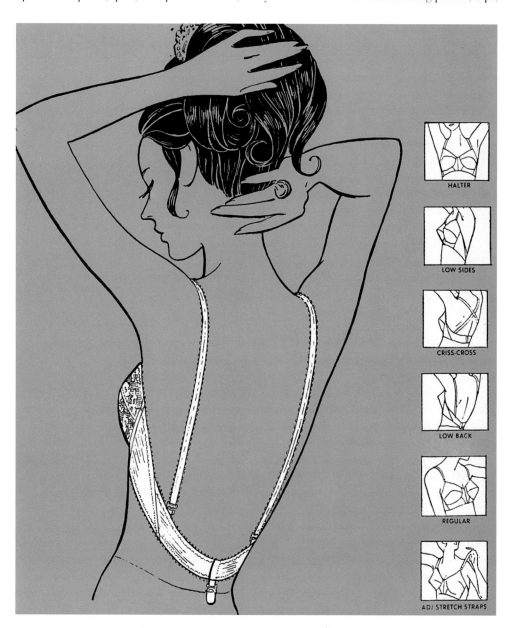

HALTER

LOW SIDES

CRISS-CROSS

LOW BACK

REGULAR

ADJ STRETCH STRAPS

The black market: Berlei's black bra and knickers (*right*) are cut in a see-through circular pattern. The cost is just as clear in this handy Berlei price list.

and belts. Bras turned up in embroidered nylon, cotton lace, net or wire, usually with padding in the cups, while bra cups were mounted with elastic to fit smugly around ribs, and straps were crossed over the back for extra support. Lace trimming and panel insets complemented each other perfectly, as did appliqués and cutouts.

Stretch support

The new breed of body-shaping bras were wire- and padding-free. While earlier models like those from Helenca featured specially-stitched padding in nylon, lace, marquisette, and elastic net, new brassières were cut in light nylon tricot. In 1964, the total control sportswear bra was introduced by Sarongster, and three years later, Formfit launched the lightest bra to date, subtly shaped in nylon and elastic and with straps which were adjustable from regular or halterneck. It was practically invisible under even the sleekest clothes.

Even the colors chosen, like the black polka dots on white on Gernreich's Exquisite Form, provoked the interests of both the wearer and of others who were fortunate enough to catch a glimpse. *Vogue* referred to the vibrant shades and psychedelic prints as a "pulse-beat brilliance" that gave the lingerie the same energy as the era it was designed in.

As the ideal figure for a woman transformed from sleek and savvy to a tall, slim, boyish shape, it was often difficult to tell the boys from the girls, except for their lingerie. Many women continued to go braless as fashion became unisex and androgynous, but others who had abandoned the bra now turned back to it for support.

Although there was a whole new range of bra styles to choose from, most were in transparent fabrics that showed off breasts in their natural shapes. At the start of the 1970s, bras were rarely rounded at the cups, some with low cleavages, narrow backs and shoulder straps; the halterneck bra was introduced in 1972. But by the middle of the decade, the rounded bra returned, with wiring to hold cutaway cups in place. Light and transparent, bras were cut in molded jersey and satin, then later in *crêpe de chine*, *mousseline*, and georgette.

As every kind of exercise became fashionable and required its own clothes, bras became more flexible in form. Even the cup edges were molded with elastic, making lingerie ready for action. A new technological process allowing curved parts of bras and girdles to be molded seamlessly from one piece of elastane, gave bras a new life. The softest bra of the decade, versatile enough to wear for any fitness activity, was designed by Christian Dior in 1971; when both the roller-skating craze and the aerobics craze evolved later in the decade, women were well prepared.

With women in the best shape they had been in for a while, the 1970s disco era was launched and satin fashions returned. Clingy dresses that fell just below the knee emphasized the body in a sensual manner, and the stretchy, comfortable bra (technically a camisole with wide straps built into the design, darted in at the bust and edged with elastic to hold it in place) was the perfect foil for these

Sheer heaven: La Perla's 1950s-style white bra (*above*) features a floral design and a see-through panel leaving less to the imagination.

Let's get physical: Easy to move in, breathe in, work in, and work out in, the new sports bras of the nineties (*left*) gave women an unparalled comfort they had never known before, welcoming them to a whole new era of lingerie.

Night magic: What turns up the heat at night more than black satin? This steamy set (*right*), designed by La Perla, is sexy enough for evening wear and a romantic rendezvous.

Lingerie in the limelight: Undergarments get overexposed as they intentionally show beneath outer fashions. A decorative Le Bourget bra (*below*) combines with a slinky dress for show-stopping appeal.

sensual looks. Satin lingerie was a hit, featuring bras and bodysuits so sleek and sexy that they were eligible to be worn on the dance floor. Glam rock prevailed, and nothing complemented designer clothes, platform shoes, and glitter makeup like a sexy bra worn in public.

Luxury in lingerie continued into the 1980s as designers turned out lingerie to complement more body-skimming fashions. Women were in hot pursuit of designer clothes, making their creators popular icons of the fashion business. Jean Paul Gaultier, Thierry Mugler, Claude Montana, and Azzedine Alaia were among the innovators of body-conscious clothing, and designers Vivienne Westwood and Jean Paul Gaultier created entire collections around bras, corsets, and basques. Lingerie followed suit with bras in sensual fabrics such as silk and satin for day and evening, like those created by designer Janet Reger, which flattered the body and were soft to wear.

Although the 1980s started with a vogue for tranquil lingerie colors, from white, flesh, coffee, black, and pinkish-mauves to embroidery in contrasting shades, adventurous colors such as burnt orange, turquoise, fuchsia, peach, apricot, pastel blue, and olive green all appeared later in the decade, often used in erotic prints and funky patterns. Bras were designed in printed cottons, printed nylon, printed jersey, and eyelet lace with panties to match.

The type of fabrics available increased, too. While fine cottons were always a staple, silk and satin imitations like Lycra silk, satin *crêpe de chine*, and polyester, equally convincing in appearance and feel, made soft lingerie more accessible and affordable. With a dedicated following of Lycra fashion, this popular fabric made its way both into dance clubs—where hiphop and break dancing moves prevailed—and onto the streets as bikerwear became a part of everyday fashion.

Spoilt for choice

Designers Comme des Garçons (whose French name, meaning "like the boys," is misleading; the fashion house was founded by Japanese designer Rei Kuwakubo) ignored the female shape altogether and developed non-figure-flattering, boyish fashions. Such clothes were well suited to the modern bra, which came with minimum, medium, and maximum control, and especially the T-shirt bra with woven cups, designed to be worn with sensible, streamlined clothes.

Other designers followed, often using underwear in their individual expressions of fashion. Jean Paul Gaultier made the bra more visible in his slashed and layered looks of 1983, before moving on to crushed velvet gowns and bustiers with foot-long pointed breasts. Yves St Laurent shortened skirts in 1985, drawing more attention to legs and breasts, and Azzedine Alaia launched his first Lycra-based fashion show in New York in 1982; his fashions were still hot in 1987 when Lycra was worn as partywear. Once again, the breasts and their silhouettes were a major fashion focus.

In the works: A machinist in the bra-making factory (*right*) shows the intricate process of bra manufacture and production.

Just peachy: A matching peach bra and knickers set (*below*) by Rigby and Peller looks pretty in a see-through peach floral pattern.

In 1992, British *Vogue* raved about the Wonderbra and sales soared. This padded, underwired push-up bra which had been introduced in Britain 30 years before had caught on once again. In 1994 the Wonderbra first appeared in Macy's department store in New York and sold more than 3000 pairs as soon as it arrived. This mega-hit was worn by women who wanted to feel empowered in the boardroom and in their personal lives.

By the late 1990s, women were involved in more sports and fitness-related endeavors than ever before. A rash of physical activity led to the creation of the sports bras of the 1990s—silhouettes with racing backs and air vents—a comfortable, unrestricting bra that was suited to its times. In the 1990s, women with complicated, busy lifestyles no longer had time to change their clothes several times a day. They want underwear that will be as suitable in the office as in the gym, in the kitchen as in the bedroom. They are spoiled for choice.

Soft at heart: A saying to swear by, this Gossard glossies advertisement (*below*) says soft is the feel of the season.

WHO SAID
A WOMAN CAN'T
GET PLEASURE
FROM SOMETHING
SOFT.

Gossard
GLOSSIES

Gossard

The history of Gossard parallels the developments in lingerie through the twentieth century, with the company responsible for many of the most significant innovations in the underwear industry. By the late 1990s, almost one hundred years after its foundation, Gossard had gained international recognition for its global marketing—with products sold in forty-five countries.

Founded in America in 1901, in Chicago, Gossard was a family business until H. W. Gossard traveled to Britain in 1921 and opened offices in London's Regent Street. Gossard, a skilled corsetière, revolutionized British foundationwear during the 1920s by introducing front-fastening corsets, a dramatic success which led to the building of a production factory in Leighton Buzzard in 1926, now the company's headquarters for its worldwide business. Gossard was set to stay.

By the 1930s, Gossard was no longer an American subsidiary, but a registered British company. Its underwear quickly gained a reputation for innovation, design, comfort, fit, and fashion, and it was Gossard which introduced the modern bra, as well as a selection of corsets using the latest art silks and elastics to suit the flowing dresses of the time. Although new products were restricted during the years of World War II—when Gossard's skilled machinists were employed in the war effort making parachutes and rubber dingies—Gossard was quick to recognize the potential of the new man-made fabrics such as nylon and incorporated them into its corsets and bras in the early 1950s. Among these were some of the first lightweight girdles, offering unprecedented comfort and fit to a generation of women who wanted to wear underwear in which they could move freely.

During the social and fashion revolutions of the 1960s, Gossard produced lingerie which appealed to women of all ages, recognizing their different desires and introducing suitable bras and corsets accordingly. For a younger generation demanding greater choice in their underwear, Gossard responded with innovative designs and patterns and introduced colorful lingerie. When the nude look became the height of fashion in the 1970s, for example, Gossard spotted a gap in the market for a bra which suggested nudity, but which provided modest cover and support. Its highly successful "Glossies" collection included seamless bras and fine, almost invisible briefs.

Power dressing of the late 1980s and the vogue for underwear as outerwear heralded Gossard's introduction of the Ultrabra in the 1990s, along with a new generation of "cleavage products." The Ultrabra Smooth featured a graduated, integral molded cup for an invisible look under the contemporary transparent fashions, while the relaunched Glossies featured in an innovative billboard advertising campaign asked the following question: "Who said a woman can't get pleasure from something soft?"

Seeing through things: Gossard's black transparent bra and matching panties (*left*) were thought out from beginning to end and are well worth the wait.

Pushing fashion over the edge: A sexy, black, tactel/satin half-cup bra (*right*) moves up on the intimate apparel essential list.

Jean-Paul Gaultier

Jean-Paul Gaultier is famous for his androgynous styling in which divisions between male and female clothing disintegrate, and become indistinguishable from each other. Sometimes known as the *enfant terrible* of the French fashion world, Gaultier was never frightened to push the boundaries of accepted fashion taste to its limits, with his personal style, his clothes, and his fashion shows all causing controversy in the 1980s and 1990s.

Jean-Paul Gaultier gained his early experience in the fashion world working as an assistant at leading haute couture houses such as Pierre Cardin, Jacques Esterel, and Jean Patou between 1970 and 1975. In 1976, the world had its taste of things to come with his first collection, an original selection of furnishings and table sets in plaited straw which caught the attention of a Japanese backer.

Within two years, the two had joined forces to present "Kashiyama" in October 1978, although the partnership soon disintegrated. Gaultier's subsequent shows featured innovative materials such as trash bags, corks, and imitation wood, in theatrical reinterpretations of earlier fashion eras. There was 1991's "French Cancan," based on the paintings of the French artist Henri de Toulouse-Lautrec, while 1995's "Riders, Horsemen of Modern Times" presented an elegant flashback to the tailcoats and stiff collars of the early 1900s.

Lingerie frequently appeared in Gaultier's work as outerwear, with his first corsets appearing in his 1983 "Dadaism" collection. Petticoats featured in his 1986 "The Dolls" show, and Gaultier launched his first dedicated lingerie for men, "Rap'Sody in Blue" in 1990, alongside his "The Rap Sisters"

The walk of fame: Jean-Paul Gaultier sends dramatic boundary-breaking pieces down the runway (*above*), stirring up bold, eclectic, sensual styles.

collection for women of bras, petticoats, panties, and underwear. Such headline-grabbing ideas captured the attention of the pop star Madonna, who commissioned Gaultier to design the costumes for her Blond Ambition World Tour in 1990. The resulting conical-shaped bra became a pop icon for a generation.

In 1992 and 1995, retrospectives of Jean-Paul Gaultier's collections were held in Los Angeles and Vienna. The income from both exhibitions was used to further AIDS research, a gesture typical of Gaultier, who used his fame and international reputation to raise awareness for other such social issues throughout the 1990s.

Corset couture: Gaultier's creative corset shapes, like the one shown here (*left*) in rose pink Lycra with top-stitched satin conical cups, drew celebrity interest. Madonna made one of his signature styles famous on a world tour.

Agent Provocateur

In 1994, Joseph Corré and his partner Serena Rees put their belief—that glamorous lingerie enhances confidence and sexuality from within—into practice, and opened Agent Provocateur in London. The shop answered a growing demand for unconventional lingerie which tantalized, but was also comfortable and exquisitely made.

The shop's interior, with its rich colors of vermilion, turquoise, and black lacquer, tasseled lanterns, rose-printed drapes, and red velvet chairs in the shape of budding flowers, was reminiscent of a chinoiserie boudoir. It was filled with lingerie that was beautiful, daring, and colorful, and before long, its regular clientele ranged from rock stars and supermodels to housewives, and businessmen.

From the start, Corré and Rees objected to the dictatorial approach of the department stores, where the selection of lingerie is limited to the offers of the major brands and the choice of the buyer governed by profit margins. At Agent Provocateur, there was something to suit everyone's taste, from waspies and waist cinchers—boned or fastened with lace, edged with satin or lace, and decorated with bows and ribbons—to bras ranging in size from a smaller 32A to a larger 38F.

Agent Provocateur's impressive array of lingerie was combined with a marketing strategy that was innovative and inventive. In 1996, an Agent Provocateur concession opened at the Fiorucci Department Store in Milan, Italy. Like the London outlet, this had jewelry from Precieux to complement the lingerie, and both were as suited to the bedroom as to the ballroom. An exclusive mail order collection was promoted in the form of collectable playing cards, featuring British pin-up girls of the 1990s, and the company joined forces with Tanqueray Gin to create a new cocktail, "The Bikini," for the launch of its provocative swimwear

Definitely daring: Whether laced up in black or printed in pink, Agent Provocateur designs (*above*) boasted to be more allure than demure.

collection. Even the shop's windows caused a sensation, featuring dominatrix sex slaves, James Bond-type girls in side-tie bikinis, and even a penis-shaped Christmas tree which was banned by the police.

The originality of Agent Provocateur lies in its stylish yet totally honest approach to lingerie as needing to be both functional and sexy, a combination of fantasy and realism evident in the creations both of Corré's mother, fashion designer Vivienne Westwood, and his father, the entrepreneurial promoter of style and fashion, Malcolm McLaren. "Throw off Puritan values, dress up, and indulge yourself in the desires of the body," says Corré. "Sex is one of the few simple pleasures in life and should be enjoyed to abandon."

A tantalizing team: Corré and Rees pose in their boudoir-inspired shop (*left*) amid a collection of lingerie pieces destined to make fashion history.

4

Panties, Briefs, and Thongs

No other clothing item has drawn such mixed reactions as panties, with which women have had a love/hate relationship since they were introduced in the late 1800s. Through the centuries women's underpants have been transformed into a key fashion essential, however, they have also been the objects of scorn and ridicule, the butt of many jokes, and the cause of embarrassment and endless giggling. They have been intimate gifts from lovers, signs of luxury, and staples in a woman's wardrobe, the most hated part of the British schoolgirl's uniform, and, when trimmed in marabou, tokens of promiscuous sex. Perhaps it is not surprising that such an all-encompassing piece of underwear should have acquired a plethora of names over the years: breeches, trousers, pantaloons, pantalettes, knickers, drawers, knickerbockers, panties, knicks, smalls, indescribables, unmentionables, bloomers, bockers, nether garments, French panties, divided skirts, step-ins, cami-panties, briefs, passion killers, and scanties.

Culotte "Vélo-Ski"

MADOR

EST INDISPENSABLE AUX SPORTIVES ÉLÉGANTES

A good briefing: a glimpse (*above*) of how panties have evolved into the styles we wear today....Shocking in color and style, more and more underwear (*right*) was shown with matching bras in daringly different looks.

In full bloom: Mrs. Bloomer's bloomers (*above*) make their mark as they pouf out the practical dress, designed by her friend Libby Miller.

The pure stuff: White knickers (*below*) with a drawstring waist and elasticized legs with lace trim feature slits up the sides and offer flexibility for exercising and cycling.

A BRIEF HISTORY

While men had worn underpants since the 1500s, women had not. The earliest underpants for women were introduced some three centuries later, typically cut with a masculine edge. These pantaloons, as they were known, were items of society women's wardrobes by 1820, but less fortunate women had to wait a while yet for affordable underpants.

The Great British Knickers—long, Turkish-style trousers, cut baggy and gathered at the ankle—were introduced in 1837 but were renamed "bloomers" in 1851 by an American, Mrs. Amelia Jenks Bloomer. Designed by Elizabeth Millers, a friend and fellow campaigner for healthier dressing, Amelia Bloomer wore the eponymous garment while speaking in London and Dublin on the subject of Reform Dress. The completely separate legs of bloomers measured 40 inches (100 cm) from the top of the waistband to the ankle, and most were modestly embroidered and trimmed around the bottom of the legs, hand-sewn with neat stitches. In early years, they were best known as *drawers*.

As the years passed, drawers became wider than ever. Made of mull muslin or silk with flounces, and often threaded with baby ribbon, they were worn under lace or silk petticoats or as frillies beneath a dress coat. Since baby ribbon and lace made panties, as they were soon called, difficult to wash, an inner lining was worn inside them. This was changed daily, or perhaps weekly, while the panties themselves were changed every three weeks or so.

As skirts narrowed, wide French panties grew impossible to wear, giving birth to skirt panties, or culottes. By the end of the century, these were generally worn under the fashionable bell-shaped skirt of the day. This was tight at the hips but was wide enough at the hem to let the wind display glimpses of white and lace. It became a thrill for men to catch

sight of the top of a woman's boots as she got on a bus—boots were also considered underclothes at the time—or a flash of her white trousers darting beneath her roomy skirt.

Embarking on a century of change

As the 1900s got underway, most panties were hand-sewn in fine cotton, cut into open styles which were some 24–28 inches (60–70 cm) wide at the knees. Such wide versions, which were also known as "free traders," were wardrobe staples for the wealthy, as were combinations, a connecting chemise and drawers. The panties were made from fine fabrics—such as those in *crêpe de chine*, torchon lace and silk bows introduced in 1909—while the most luxurious close-fitting combinations were made out of wool silk or plain ribbed knits.

Skirts grew so narrow and long in the early century that a woman's thighs were practically squeezed together—she could only move from the knees down when she walked, and they hid everything right down to the boots. As a result, the traditional slit at the crotch in panties gradually disappeared in the design of luxury underwear, although it remained standard in rural and poverty-stricken areas. The Hobble Skirt, revived from the mid-1890s and reintroduced to the fashion world in 1911 by the French couturier Paul Poiret, made more practical versions of panties acceptable, as did other slender styles.

Women began to appropriate men's clothing for the first time—the first item inspired by the male wardrobe, the serge knickerbocker suit, became standard wear for those on bicycles—and in 1913, a bicycling dress, a combination of a jacket and divided skirt, or knickerbockers, of grayish-brown twill worn with cotton liners was introduced. This garment became a sporting woman's staple and was referred to as "rationals," but although it was an advance for the freedom of women, it was also marked with the stigma of sober Reform Dress. Many, many women of the day were not in favor of emancipation, fearing the loss of their traditional passive roles, and they longed for the real frills that symbolized true femininity.

"Rationals" were also worn by women who engaged in routine exercise regimes, although movement was difficult in these inflexible fabrics that also could not breathe. It required the craze for dances such as the tango and charleston to introduce a new sense of freedom, and before long, tango

If can-can girls can wear them, so can the rest of us. It was customary to catch a glimpse of these lacy lingerie looks (*below*) when sky-high kicks were the highlight of the show.

Thanks to similarly flexible underpinnings, Señorita Castora de Guilter and Monsieur Giore (*left*) perform the Argentine tango at the Comedy Theatre in suitable attire.

panties were born. These turned up in exotic, black sarsenet (fine soft silk), trimmed with lace frills and cut roomy so the wearer could complete the required strides of the dance. They were formed from one length of material which fell from the waist in front to the knees and up again to the waist at the back with slits at the sides for legs.

Preparing for war

Within a decade or so, glimpses of petticoats and drawers were frequently visible at the beach where girls changed publicly, on tiered seats at the circus, and at sports stadiums. They could also be glimpsed during certain sporting events, such as tennis and cycling, where they peeked out from under short skirts. These instances always caused a stir, as underclothes had simply not been seen in public before 1900.

Drawers and panties were now practically interchangeable, and popular versions included "golf panties" of white cotton or linen, drawers with a buttoned flap at the back and wide frilled legs (available in Britain through Army & Navy store catalogs as early as 1912), and woolen drawers which were longer and close-fitting. Fleecy-lined short panties debuted that same year, as did wide, frilly-legged French panties. Close-fitting panties that closed with elastic or bands at the knees and waist were also worn, known as *directoire* knickers. These had a detachable lining in white stockinette and with a button flap at the back.

But by 1914, with the outbreak of World War I, European women needed freedom of movement to work in the war effort. Those that joined the Volunteer Aid Detachment (VAD) to nurse on battlegrounds in France and elsewhere wore uniforms, and as a result, knicker lengths were shortened to 21 inches (53 cm) and legs were widened to a circumference of 38 inches (96.5 cm). World War I had other influences on knicker design, too. Troops returning to Britain after serving in India under Lord Seymour brought home transparent silk gauze garments for their women and named them *see-mores*.

As peace returned to Europe, woven panties in various colors, such as those with colored hems in tangerine or lemon advertised in women's magazines in 1920, became popular. Underwear with designs of birds and flowers appeared, most cut in *crêpe de chine* with closed elastic waists. By the mid-1920s, the chemise and panties were often combined in all-in-ones, while contemporary swimsuits with legs or frilled skirts hid attached panties underneath. Some knicker combinations featured an attached shaped bra in yellow, blue, violet, rose, or jade, with gold net or cream lace decorating the chiffon base, or made from black *crêpe de chine* for a daring evening ensemble.

Just in the knick of time…women who yearned for freedom from laced-up bloomers and an easier way of dressing were thrilled with the concept of the cami-knicker (*above*)—a camisole and knicker combination.

Going graphic: Black cami-knickers (*right*) take on a graphic edge as a white ribbon is stitched onto the front fabric covering the breasts. The slit in the middle makes them easy to move in.

Fancier fabrics: Thanks to new synthetic fabrics in the '40s, knickers (*above*) came in all different cuts and styles.

Cami-knickers featuring flaps that buttoned together at the middle of the thighs were introduced, allowing women to feel naked and free while maintaining some level of respectability. But the satin panties offered little protection under the short hemlines of flapper dresses that were in vogue, and most women thought they lacked modesty and grace. Before long, such underwear was transformed into close-fitting panties, but these first tight-fitting knickers had one big drawback—the fabrics they were made from.

Women sweated out this fashion trend in itchy wool and thick denim, held in place with tight elastic, and had to wear each pair for a few weeks at a time since the materials were so difficult to wash. Nonetheless, they continued to be a staple of the underwear wardrobe, and underwear designers focused their efforts on how to smooth out lingerie lines under stylish outergarments. It was agreed that creaseless perfection could only be achieved by wearing a minimum of clothing beneath the outer clothes, but, asked *Vogue* in 1924, "What would our grandmothers have thought of limiting their evening dress to a pair of panties?"

By the mid-1930s, sturdy little cotton briefs were finally adopted by women of all backgrounds, considered more sexy than black lace. They had got used to the feel of their bare skin under their other clothes, and combinations which women wore over their bras and panties slowly disappeared. Like earlier panties, these were considered old-fashioned and were not suitable for sports or leisure wear. A minimal number of underwear pieces was preferred, and by the time World War II loomed at the end of the decade, a bra, briefs, and garter (suspender) belt had become the main undergarment staples for most women.

The effects of war

During World War II, rationing on both sides of the Atlantic meant that lingerie of all types became far more austere. In Britain, it took three ration coupons to buy a pair of panties, and many women believed that the only way to have feminine undies was to make them yourself. All kinds of garments, including panties and cami-knickers, were knitted from "Stitchcraft" patterns and home sewing kits, while old clothes were unpicked and revamped into underwear.

By the early 1940s, panties were small, cut away at the front or sides over the upper thighs for ease of movement, some with elasticized sides that combined the roles of panties and corset. Those cut on a bias in jersey gave the best fit, and when the land army of French women were asked to choose between lace panties and jersey briefs as the most appropriate underwear for women, they opted for jersey briefs, which were more practical and less enticing. The few simple undergarments that were worn aroused no interest at all in the wearer or their admirers, although the walls where servicemen bunked were cluttered with pin-up girls on calendars wearing very little; underwear could no longer be considered an unmentionable.

Nylon had been patented and was in production just before the outbreak of World War II, at which time DuPont used it to make stockings. Its use was then restricted until after 1945 to the war effort, during which time the revolutionary new material was turned into rope, tents, parachutes, and other vital supplies. Damaged parachutes (made of silk or later nylon) were occasionally released to the public for recycling, and many of the triangular strips that formed the chute were reconstructed into underwear—although wedding dresses would occasionally take priority. One British wedding *trousseau* of 1944 included French panties made from nylon parachute pieces and decorated with a side button and Buckinghamshire lace, although they were dense and excruciatingly hot to wear.

Women in the British Armed Services wore panties in dreary uniform colors: khaki, navy, blue/gray, and black. These uniform panties were dubbed passion killers, ETBs (elastic tops and bottoms), boy bafflers, wrist catchers, and taxi cheaters, and were not elegant. The traditional *directoire* style was necessary under the regulation knee-length skirts of 1941, and most of the

The first silk look-alikes

The 1920s brought hope for a solution to the problem of itchy, uncomfortable fabrics so close to the skin as man-made imitation silks were developed by fabric companies. One such example, artificial silk, or "art silk," was first commercially produced by the American Viscose Company in 1910, and was manufactured from wood pulp, corn protein, and chemical compounds. Rayon was another, used by the French couturier Gabrielle "Coco" Chanel as early as 1915 for a collection of model gowns. But it was among working-class girls who could now indulge in fashions previously reserved for the rich that these fabrics found their market, cut into downmarket versions of luxurious lingerie.

Design virtuoso: Coco Chanel (1883-1971) set up her own couture house and created the famous brand of perfume Chanel No. 5 in 1929.

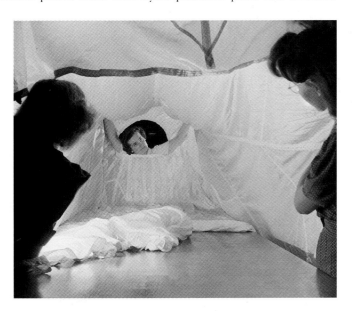

Life-saving undergarments: Defective parachutes couldn't save the lives of men in combat but when transformed into pairs of women's knickers (*left*), many women could breathe sighs of relief.

fabric used for regulation underwear was coarse and uncomfortable. Black panties made in 1945 from an artificial lock-knit material in dark navy or black were loathed and seldom worn. Children suffered, too, pressed into frocks over matching panties in floral cottons for summer and into coarse gray mohair tweed, which was hatefully itchy to wear, in winter. Such styles lasted virtually unchanged from World War I right into the mid-1950s.

Within two years of the war's end, in 1945, Christian Dior, the French fashion designer, launched his famous, opulent New Look. He recreated a pleasingly curved, cinch-waisted woman who wore long full skirts and frothy underwear, a far cry from the tweed-clad women who had been coping with war. Under the yards of material that made up the skirts, women wore panties and briefs of nylon, following its invention in the late 1930s.

Knickers were still designed in the French style, but many of the tough, young women who grew up during the war years favored briefs, manufactured in plain and printed nylon and acetate materials, and often trimmed with nylon frills or lace. British Nylon Spinners, a British company granted a nylon patent in 1939, developed Bri-nylon, a famous trade name in the late 1940s and 1950s, and clothes stores quicky became filled with drip-dry, easy-care underwear.

Briefs grew even briefer until there was virtually no material left to them at all. The simple G-string, a single thin string which was worn as an elastic strip around the waist and up the backside of the wearer, was originally the basis of a stripper's wardrobe, but was brought into the mainstream by specialty shops and mail order catalogs. Frederick's of Hollywood, in the daring underwear business since 1946, manufactured G-strings with pockets and teeny-weeny split crotch bikinis that were meant to be fun. Taking the entertainment concept one step further, a Californian company marketed the Incredible Edible Candy-pants in a wild cherry flavor.

Nylon was the news in the 1940s, as fashion's newest texture took over the undergarment world, making lingerie (*above*) easier to care for and more comfortable to wear.

In full swing...actress Marilyn Monroe (*right*) gives the world a show of her brightest briefs while standing over a sidewalk grating in the motion picture, "*The Seven Year Itch*."

Sweet success...the ingenious Incredible Edible underwear company introduces its savory silhouette, the Candy-pants (*below*).

Black lace, which had been around since the sixteenth century, first became popular in the late 1800s and was named after the French town of Chantilly where much of it was made. But by the early twentieth century, hand- or machine-made black lace had become the essential ingredient of seductive underwear, and was still worn by chorus girls in the 1940s, trimmed with electric blue satin ribbons. White lace was a different matter, although the American tennis player Gussie Moran shocked Wimbledon in 1949 when audiences caught more than a glance of her eye-catching, frilly lace panties designed by Teddy Tinling.

Stretching the boundaries

With the 1950s arrived a range of soft natural and synthetic materials, including a host of elasticized fabrics that were quickly incorporated into lingerie, and advertising campaigns of the time portrayed a variety of styles and colors. Skirts got shorter in 1953, the fullest imitating earlier crinolines, but under them women wore briefs and garter (suspender) belts, or girdles that were closed between the legs. Open girdles, worn either over briefs or on their own with no briefs at all, were also popular.

Respectable names like Montfort, Woollaton, Alpine Interlock, Bairnswear, Qualesta, Chilprufe, Cosicura, and Puritex Hygienic were among the leading brands sold in department stores, which also stocked a good supply of cami-knickers. One particularly elegant design came from Duvelleray, whose beautifully-shaped cami-knickers of peach lace had narrow bindings, shoulder straps, and a shaped inset of peach satin.

But it was Hollywood that really revealed what women were wearing. "There is no film star today whose underwear we have not seen," once said Sophia Loren, and women rushed to follow their lead. Movies, and later television, let the world know how celebrities and socialites dressed, and stars became famous for their figures and underwear, or lack of it. Mae West's hourglass physique was legendary, as were those of Marilyn Monroe and Jean Harlow, among many others.

As the front line in the struggle to shape and restrain the body, panties of all types were particularly influenced by the introduction of Lycra in the mid-1960s. With all of the qualities of elastic but far more adaptable, Lycra was a powerful weapon in the lingerie arsenal. Briefs previously cut from stretch fabrics such as nylon tricot offered more support when made in Lycra and lace.

As the 1960s progressed, women only wanted undergarments which were simple and functional, made with synthetic fabrics that needed no ironing, were easily washed, and fitted any shape. They displayed a revolution in taste, opting for pantyhose, or tights, which covered their lower limbs and the area of the thighs which had traditionally been left bare, and stretch panties were popular as they flattened the stomach and were promoted as helping the wearer lose over 1 pound (2.2 kilos) in weight.

Fashion magazines showed gorgeous toned bodies in clothing that required no underwear at all—or perhaps just mini bikini panties and pantyhose. There was a feeling, at least among those with younger, firmer bodies, that artificially molded flesh was corrupt, although the less daring moved on to lingerie that was both sensual and functional.

Following in the footsteps of the designer

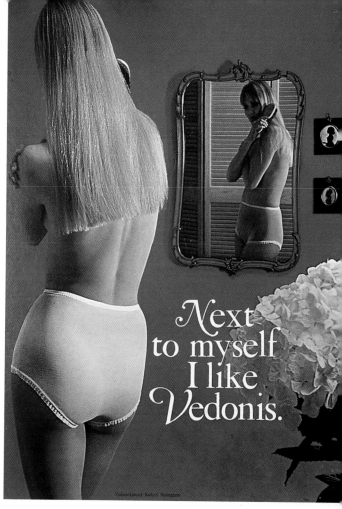

Next to myself I like Vedonis.

In brief...panties (*above*) grew sleeker and slimmer and were cut closer to the body, soon to be thought of by most women as second skins.

What's your fancy? La Perla's 1960s knitted matching bra and knickers (*below*) feature a decorative bow at the front.

The everyday look: A woman in the '60s (*above*) combs her hair in front of the mirror wearing nothing but her knickers as part of her everyday routine.

Ladies first: A pair of brown French knickers (*right*) with cream lace trim gives these undergarments feminine flare.

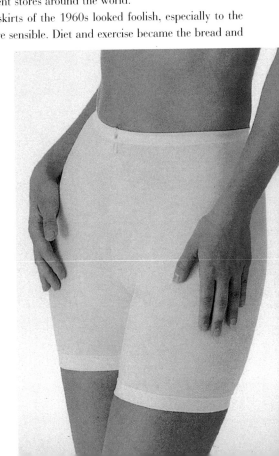

Lucille, lingerie designer Janet Reger correctly judged the mood of underwear in London to launch her highly successful luxury lingerie shops. In 1964, Barbara Hulanicki, another designer, started a small mail-order business based on images of Hollywood vamps. Her designs were imaginative and sexy in dark smudgy colors and fluid materials, and so successful that she opened the first Biba boutique in Kensington, a fashionable area of London.

As women's outer clothes, and especially the miniskirt, became increasingly short, undies had to be sleek and figure-hugging. Popular bikini pants turned up in stretch nylon yarn with bright colors—lime, pink, purple, and orange—and strong patterns. In the search for machine-washable fabrics, polyester, Banlon, and Lycra were the most highly sought after materials, although paper panties were manufactured in 1969 to eliminate any washing at all. They set the scene for the throwaway consumerism that society was about to embrace, although their appeal waned by the mid 1970s.

Selling sensuality

A minority of women still preferred traditional white or pastel underwear, and some turned to expensive designer makes such as those created by Janet Reger. Her silk and lace designs provided high-society customers with the revived charms of seductive feminine underclothes, anticipating the vogue for tailored, close-fitting, and sensual lingerie in the 1970s.

Frilly knickers, knee-length petticoats, low-cut and long-line bras, and French knickers in sensuous silks all came and went during the 1970s. Reger launched a line of knickers that were flattering to wear for evening or day in soft, pale pink satin and cream lace, while her cami-knickers decorated the body instead of dressing it. The French lingerie designer Sabbia Rosa displayed her high-quality underwear from 1976 onward, and within five years, her creations made their debut in major department stores around the world.

Suddenly the see-through blouses and micro skirts of the 1960s looked foolish, especially to the youth movement which had grown older and more sensible. Diet and exercise became the bread and butter of fashion magazines which supported trim, well-toned bodies, but nonetheless, hemlines dropped, leaving the covered leg to the imagination of the observer.

Partially-clothed bodies were enhanced by the sensuous new fabrics incorporated into intimate and specialty lingerie. Transparent nylon blouses with satin pants edged in machine lace and ultralight camisoles were fun to wear

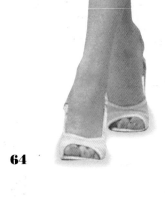

Underwear becomes outerwear as designers turn out see-through pieces (*left*) with a seriously sensual edge. Suddenly, the body is in the spotlight and everything that is worn is meant to flaunt it.

Designed to celebrate a sleek body and lend a helping hand to those that need a little tweaking, Wacoal created this panty slimmer (*right*) of polyester and Lycra to wear under skirts, pants and dresses.

Freedom in fashion was the signature trait of Mary Quant's designs. Her matching bra and underwear set (*right*) sends steamy signals down every wearer's spine.

Leggings, thermals and biker shorts (*far right*) are the latest generation of knicker fashion. Designed for freedom of movement in sports, exercise and everyday life, they are just a hint of newer knicker revelations to come.

and sexy for him to remove, as were front-closing bras, slips, G-strings, and teddies that encouraged sexual fantasies. The consumers for these daring lingerie looks were women who felt sexually liberated but who wanted to feel seductive. They provided a huge market for eroticism, which expanded even more toward the end of the decade and through the '80s and '90s.

Catering for all tastes

No market represented the 1970s as powerfully as that of the exercise and sportswear mania, however, and as the fitness craze became a cult, lingerie took on a decidedly functional mode. In 1984, the American designer Calvin Klein took the unisex T-shirt and jeans one step further and decided that men and women could share knickers—his famous jockey shorts for women were bestsellers for years to come—but by the 1980s, women were in search of form, function, fun, and frivolity.

A plethora of silk and satin French knickers edged in lace were on offer, worn under evening dresses, and bras and knickers made in matching sets were everywhere. As the 1990s approached, a large swathe of undergarments were no longer referred to as underwear, lingerie, or undies but as intimate apparel, a name that conjured up images of romantic luxury.

Other underwear took on a lighthearted note—whimsical briefs were created in red, white, and blue nylon as Independence Day souvenirs, and white knickers boasting plastic eyes and a big red fluffy nose were sold as gag gifts—while a range of new thermal fabrics were developed in response to the much-developed outdoor adventure industry. Thermal underwear made the most of a manufacturing process where air is trapped in small cells, holding the body's own heat between the material and skin to keep the wearer warm in winter.

Leading manufacturers of thermal fabrics realized they were onto something. Damart, an underwear mail-order company specializing in winter warmers developed thermolactyl, a mixture of synthetic and natural fibers, while Wolsey's warming products were cut in pure wool and cashmere for luxury garments. Marks & Spencer's feminized long johns were sought out by the fashionable and winter warriors.

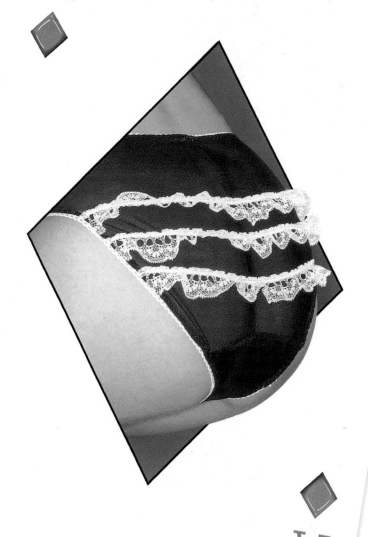

After a century of evolution, knickers had transformed themselves by the late 1990s. What had started as voluminous bloomers in rough, scratchy fabrics had slimmed down to panties, briefs, and thongs, the staple of every woman's day and evening wardrobes. The taboo on seeing or mentioning "smalls" had long passed, replaced by catalog upon catalog of intimate apparel in any number of man-made fabrics. Simplicity of line had replaced modesty, color the starched white cotton of earlier times.

Mystery in the making: Agent Provocateur's black knickers (*right*) with three layers of white lace on the back create an especially alluring look.

Gruppo La Perla

Gruppo La Perla, one of the largest fashion houses in Italy, distributes its exquisitely styled, luxurious lingerie, swimwear, and perfume throughout the world, in some of the most prestigious department stores including Harrods in London and Saks, Neiman Marcus, and Bergdoff Goodman in New York; as well as Takishimaya and Wako in Japan, El Corte Inglés in Spain, Galeries Lafayette in France, and El Palacio de Hierro in Mexico. The company made its reputation by designing for elegant, sophisticated modern women who enjoy the confidence that La Perla's sought-after under and outerwear inspire.

Seduction at its best: Men have no choice but to surrender to a woman in this getup (*above*). The black lace basque is fastened to thigh-high stockings with black suspender belts.

The company was founded in 1954 by the Italian designer Ada Masotti. Working from a small workshop in Bologna, a city celebrated for its sophisticated textile industry, Masotti started out by using the highest quality fabrics to create fine underwear. She understood and anticipated women's desires, designing a selection of lingerie that perfectly enhanced Christian Dior's New Look, the fashion of the day.

During its development, and under the direction of Dr. Alberto Masotti, Ada Masotti's son who joined in the company in the 1960s, Gruppo La Perla built up a reputation for lingerie that was distinctive for its beautifully crafted styling. Much of it featured handmade lace and embroidery, crafted into a range that included separates, delicate chemises, petticoats, and negligées.

In the 1980s, La Perla launched its Malizia collection and followed this with a raunchy range under the Marvel brand name. Its success in the lingerie market encouraged Gruppo La Perla to diversify, and the company turned its attention to such products as swimwear and perfume. Its luxury swimwear, marketed as La Perla Mare, and its outerwear collections carrying the labels Ritmo di Perla and Io La Perla for couture, were all manufactured in one of three factories in Bologna, Italy, each of which specialized in one line. The La Perla fragrance was manufactured under

license in Parma.

In the 1990s, Gruppa La Perla opened a number of dedicated boutiques in cities renowned for their fashionable shopping districts. In Paris, there is a La Perla on the Faubourg St Honoré, London's "Sculpture," on Brook Street, Mayfair, is dedicated to the La Perla collection, and in 1994 a La Perla store opened on Madison Avenue, New York. There are boutiques in Venice, Barcelona, Hong Kong, and Tokyo. The success of this worldwide marketing strategy was undeniable, as by the mid to late 1990s, the company employs more than 2,000 people, with an annual turnover in excess of 250 million dollars. At least ten more La Perla boutiques will open by the year 2000.

The lady in white: She'll stop traffic in this pretty white cardigan and slip with matching bra (*left*).

Sloggi

In less than twenty years, Sloggi took the world by storm. Making the most of recent advances in the man-made material Lycra, the German corset company Triumph lived up to its name with its tight-fitting, long-lasting cotton/Lycra mix underpants, which stylishly adorned bottoms around the world throughout the 1980s and 1990s. Suddenly, smalls were big business.

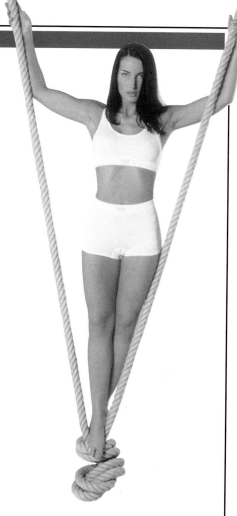

Hip-hugging and happening: A white Lycra ribbed top and shorts, showing the Sloggi logo (*above*) ensure shapes that don't lose their cool.

The company was founded almost one hundred years earlier, in 1886, by the Germans Gottfried Spiesshofer and Michael Braun. In 1902, they took Triumph as the company's registered trademark, and by 1930 Triumph had become the largest corset maker in Europe. Having built up subsidiary companies throughout Europe and the Far East, Triumph set up a dedicated lingerie division in 1966.

Through the 1970s, Triumph International developed and patented a special fabric called Corespun. To make this, Lycra thread was wrapped with cotton, a technique which created, when woven, a comfortable, soft, and stretchy fabric in which only cotton is next to the skin of the wearer. This was the fabric that was used in the Sloggi collection, made of 95% cotton and 5% Lycra, the combination ensuring that Sloggi briefs retained their perfect shape and figure-hugging fit no matter how many times they were washed: They could withstand temperatures of up to 200°F (95° C).

The fabric was perfect, but the company had no name for their new product. History relates that after the marketing department had racked their brains for a brand name to no avail, they gathered a heap of letters, and tossed them in the air. When they landed on the floor, the name Sloggi appeared.

The first Sloggi briefs were the Classic range of basics, consisting of just four styles—Maxi, Midi, Mini, and Tanga. Initially Sloggi briefs were only available in white, but other colors such as black and gray were soon introduced to meet demand. All the models were figure-hugging and provided an immediate solution to the knicker taboo, "VPL," or visible panty line.

As briefs gained fashion status in the early 1980s, logos appeared on the waistbands of men's underwear. The Sloggi 100 range was launched in 1983 with an integral Sloggi logo on the underpants waistband. The brand gained designer-label status among younger customers who wanted sportswear rather than lingerie. Another line, the 100, was created for this market, with its string, the Tai (a cross between a string and a tanga), and a soft bra.

In 1991, Triumph International decided that men should be able to enjoy Sloggi fit and comfort, and introduced Sloggi for Men in seven different styles. Simultaneously the company was working on a more luxurious line for women. Sloggi Luxe retained the Corespun fabric but included lace inserts at the sides of a selection of six pantie styles, and also expanded into a soft and underwired bra, a body, and four different tops.

Sloggi Control appeared in 1995, a natural progression at a time when many manufacturers were turning their attention to lingerie that shaped the figure and provided uplift for the bottom. Soon after, the launch of the Sloggi 200 and 300 lines reinforced the brand's position as the world's leading pantie, with the Sloggi logo highly visible on the waistband. In addition to its own logo, Sloggi 300 featured a tubular knit waistband without seams and a longer gusset with a double layer of towelling, both designed for even greater comfort.

Sloggi's marketing even affected the way that customers perceived and purchased panties. Sold individually and in multipacks, Sloggi's distinctive packaging—at one time, its advertising featured Snow White and the Seven Drawers—stood out on the shelves of leading department stores throughout the 1990s. Sloggi's success had turned panties into fast-moving consumer goods. By the late 1990s, Triumph International had sold over 400 million pieces around the world, inadvertently changing the whole concept of briefs in the process. Despite this massive output, Sloggi's quality never faded. The briefs retained their reputation for comfort, fit, form, and fabric, appealing to women (and men) of all ages.

Marks & Spencer

Marks & Spencer, the British retail chain affectionately referred to as "M&S," sells approximately 1.5 million pairs of "knickers" every week—roughly two pairs every second. Not surprisingly, it is calculated that almost every woman in Britain owns a pair of the company's knickers, not to mention their bras (of which they sell over 300,000 a week, a massive 15.6 million bras per year), and tights (some 600,000 pairs per week).

The business was formed in 1894 by Michael Marks and Tom Spencer, although it was not until the 1920s that hosiery appeared on the company's inventory lists. Early items were mostly camisoles and bloomers, sold to customers who associated Marks & Spencer with thrift, value, and quality.

Michael Mark's original slogan had been, "Don't ask the price—it's a penny." The company's low prices were the result of trading direct with manufacturers for cash, a principle, if not the prices, which remains unchanged to this day. Marks & Spencer's goods are immediately recognizable by their "St Michael" trademark, which first appeared on "pajamas and knitted articles of clothing" back in 1928. The trademark soon became an absolute assurance to customers of high-quality, well-designed merchandise "at reasonable prices," as set out in the principles of the business philosophy.

Another core principle of the early business was to "encourage suppliers to use the most modern and efficient techniques of production provided by the latest discoveries in science and technology," thus explaining Marks & Spencer's ability to develop and promote new products. A direct result of such collaboration was the invention of a machine for attaching straps to lingerie, replacing skilled sewing machinists with semiskilled loaders and, as a result, vastly increasing the company's output.

Marks & Spencer was among the first shops to offer Art Silk items. The success of the low-cost "Artificial Silk Rayon Knicker" led to Art Silk underwear and nightwear in the 1930s, from nightdresses, pajamas, and

Intricate details: Marks & Spencer thought of everything from machines that attach straps to fabric to trimmings of white/cream lace when designing this frilly frock (*left*).

Touting high tech: Marks & Spencer utilized advanced technology to create cutting-edge classics—here, their flower patterned bra and knickers (*right*) get a dose of M&S genius.

dressing gowns to French knickers, camiknickers, and slips. During World War II, its close links with many of the lingerie manufacturers meant that Marks & Spencer was the ideal company to head the British Government's Utility Scheme. It developed a selection of clothing combining its "St Michael" trademark with the Utility label.

Post-war production

Following the end of the war in 1945, Marks & Spencer, like other underwear manufacturers, was soon making widespread use of nylon. The first nylon slips, briefs, and nightgowns were offered on a sale-or-return basis in 1949, and by 1954, the company offered twenty-seven different types of nylon slips, featuring "superior lace design" and "trimmed appliqué on lace."

Adapting to the changes in outerwear during the 1960s, Marks & Spencer encouraged new production techniques and materials, including crocheted elastics to produce neater edges. Simultaneously, it developed new cottons, improved satins, and experimented with chiffons and georgettes, as well as more decorative items and colors.

Lycra was to have a major impact on lingerie in the 1980s, but it had already appeared in the Marks & Spencer Waistline Brassière as early as 1970. As Lycra developed, Marks & Spencer combined it with natural fibers such as cotton for comfortable, close-fitting panties. Because of the revolutionary impact of the new fiber, designers working for the company could

experiment ever more widely, soon resulting in the highleg cut on briefs and swimwear. Before long, matching sets of bras and briefs were on sale, taking their bras out of traditional boxed packaging and displaying them on hangers close to the matching highlegs. Indeed, it was during the 1980s that Marks & Spencer underwear really took off, with enormous areas of their stores devoted to fashion-led lingerie and hosiery.

Quintessentially a British retailer, Marks & Spencer expanded overseas from 1975 onward, with huge success.

The St Michael brand gained international recognition, with customers from every age and income bracket. By the late 1990s, there were 566 Marks & Spencer stores worldwide—spreading through Europe, the Far East and the Pacific Basin—with an additional eighty-five St Michael franchises. Marks & Spencer's American expansion has taken place through the Brooks Brothers' chain of clothing retailers, which it acquired in 1988.

5

The Body and Sportswear

Before the mid 1800s, very few respectable women took part in any form of sporting activity, which was considered a masculine domain. Women with a passion for athletics had to struggle for the right to exercise in public, and those who rode horseback—for sport and travel purposes—wore some form of riding habit, or divided skirt; which originated from those worn by the South American gauchos. Pants or trousers were generally frowned upon for women—police in Germany issued regulations against them—although they were considered acceptable on the ski slopes. But

such attitudes were soon to pass, as within twenty-five years, sports clothes were worn by all and sundry, and before a century had passed, sports clothes had become everyday wear.

During the 1970s, the body stocking, a natural extension of the elasticized, fitted Lycra leotards of the early 1970s, took the clothes world by storm. They were worn as disco and roller-skating attire; with funky skirts, shorts, and leotards, and under tiny-waisted ballgowns. Exercise leotards, stretch bodysuits, and antique lingerie were all worn as evening clothes in a time when designer labels became status symbols. By the end of the century, skintight stretchwear was as chic as you could get.

Pretty underpinnings: Lacy bloomers (*above*) became standard underclothes for women and avid exercisers were able to get even more mileage out of the Edwardian look.

A SPORTING REVOLUTION

Bicycling and skating both became popular pastimes for women at the end of the 1800s, and as women's corsets were eliminated, bloomers became commonplace. Bloomers, billowing trousers derived from the dress of Turkish women and named for their nineteenth-century advocate Amelia Bloomer, were an early attempt at sensible dressing. They were frowned upon at first, but men and women soon realized they were necessary for participation in certain sports. Before long the gym suit as hated by generations of British schoolgirls was born, at first full-length and then shortened. Finally it went undercover, and was termed underwear.

While croquet could be played by tightly-laced women in a corset and knickers, active sports required a completely different kind of outfit. The demise of multiple petticoats and corsets was inevitable as hems grew shorter, skirts were divided, and elasticized fabrics were developed. Early sporting outfits were adapted from the fashionable styles of daily wear, as seen by Hollywood director Mack Sennett's early cinematic bathing beauties, who wore stockings, bloomers, long jersey tunics, shoes, and mop caps. The famous French tennis champion, Suzanne Lenglen—dressed by the French couturier Paul Poiret—was thought shocking when she first wore a simple pleated knee-length dress with firmly gartered white stockings to play in the early 1920s. By 1926, lingerie was cut at its narrowest yet, albeit with frivolous additions that gave women the feeling they were on the path to beauty. The 1927 Miss America Beauty contest showed how the slow change in idealized body types had taken hold: contestants appeared taller, leaner, and fitter as a result of their participation in active sports, wearing bathing suits with more revealing lines.

The advantage of stretch

As early as the 1930s, the body began to peek out from underneath its covering of clothing. Lingerie shapes emphasized a woman's hourglass shape, clinging to the body, hips, and breasts with elasticized fabrics. An all-in-one girdle and brassière of 1937 was typical, still lightly boned and high waisted, while slips were fitted and heavily ornamented with lace.

The image of the body was strongly affected by the production of nylon by DuPont in 1938. This strong but lightweight fabric was woven or knitted by machine in various deniers (weights), washed easily, and required only drip drying instead of ironing. For sportswear, the new nylon was included in tricot knickers, which were similar to trunks, and the sports skirt. Companies such as Rosy included elasticized materials that molded the body in its lingerie. Indeed, lingerie became increasingly flexible as women began to take part in more and more sports, especially after the end of World War II in 1945. They now played tennis, rode, and skied in

Surf's up: The new stretch fabrics (*left*) made it easier for girls to play. Soon-to-come water-repellent clothing would later up the fun factor.

Tennis, anyone? In the '20s, players wore clothes from head to toe. Mary K. Brown (*left*), America's opponent to France's Suzanne Lenglen, wears a long-sleeved top and skirt as she perfects her swing.

A plethora of pleats: 1947 swimsuits (*above*) get trimmed with ruffles thanks to a treatment called ruching which uses pleats to form gathered edges of material.

increasing numbers, and bras and girdles made from elasticized fabrics were produced in quantity. Silk, cotton shantung, net satin, and brocade, and later all forms of nylon such as power net, taffeta, satin, and chiffon mesh, made the most of the figure.

Communication between America and Europe was disrupted during World War II, and the fashion connection between the two was severed, too. As a result, Americans developed their own styles and manufacturing processes—which stood them in good stead once the war ended—but they missed the influence of France's couturiers. Things looked up after 1945, especially when the Paris designer Christian Dior introduced his New Look for Spring 1947. This made the most of the feminine figure, with prominent breasts, small waists, and rounded hips and buttocks. His style restored a sensuality to dress which had been lost during the austere war years, despite the emergence of the female navel, which was suddenly on display in 1943 in magazine advertisements for belly button contests. It was the bikini, born in the 1940s, which opened the way for such exposure.

In 1949, tennis star Gussie Moran shocked audiences at Wimbledon with her eye-catching Teddy Tinling frilly panties. Worn under a short dress, and more provocative than knickers, the frilly panties led the way for other innovative tennis fashion stars. In the mid-1950s, Helen Jacobs became the first woman to wear shorts at Wimbledon, a revolution in itself in a decade which gave rise to many such changes in sportswear.

Hit the beach: In the 1950s, beachwear (*below*) came in the form of halter tops and bikini briefs for women with cover-ups to match. Men's swimwear followed suit.

The influence of dance

Much earlier in the century, just as much had been revealed by the hugely popular *cancan* and strip shows. In these, bloomers were worn as outer clothes while lingerie that was far less substantial was commonplace. In France, bawdy *cancan* dancers, many of whom were originally laundresses and other working women, kicked high to reveal their stockings, garters, petticoats, and sometimes more. Glimpses of bare flesh at the tops of their hose were considered racy and tantalizing in a culture where skirts reached the floor and undergarments were worn in multiple layers. Such exotic dancers were symbols of a debauched nightlife and the people who lived it. French artists such as Henri Toulouse-Lautrec depicted the hectic atmosphere of the Music Hall, illustrating both the dancers and prostitutes who frequented them. Edgar Degas was also fascinated by such dancers, picturing them in brothels in various states of undress.

Just as the tango dance craze of the early 1900s led to the first brassière and the

abandoning of the whalebone corset, so the dance revolution of the 1950s instigated some radical changes in underwear. By the 1950s, as censorship of the arts was gradually relaxed, European and American fashions were growing much sexier, as was the music of the day. There was plenty of dancing going on during these years, as early rock 'n' roll swept first through North America and then across to Europe.

The dance craze was huge, and dancers wanted fewer and lighter clothes, not always choosing them for their practicality. Women who had been bound up all day in corsets or stiff suits and dresses wanted to let loose at night. Nightspots demanded minimalist, body-conforming clothes that moved with the dancer and required a minimum of lingerie. (Later dances such as the jitterbug, the shimmy, the twist, the hustle, and hip hop similarly required their own underclothing.) More formal ballroom dancers like Irene Castle and Ginger Rogers showed off their high-style elegance with the beautiful, supple lingerie they wore under their floating gowns.

It was an era of new fundamental fashion, fashion that flowed in a fluid line, showing off the natural curves of the body which were smoothed or controlled with light elastic lingerie. Slim waists were popular, often achieved with the help of an all-in-one corselette, and haute couture designers such as Christian Dior, Jacques Fath, Pierre Balmain, and the House of Lanvin delved into the creation of underwear and casualwear using new artificial fibers and fabrics. Bulges visible under dancing dresses, as well as slacks and tight blue jeans, were smoothed away with panty girdles which were much like elasticized shorts. One, a lightweight elastic net girdle with a double tummy panel created by Meerson Fairbell in 1957, was rumored to be invisible under clothes. Such girdles were briefer and more flexible than ever before, and began to turn up in a variety of vivid colors, such as sapphire blue, that made the skin look pure and fresh.

Dance fever: In the 1950s rock 'n roll era, women were kicking up their heels on the dance floor in body-skimming clothes (*above*). Showing off seductive underwear was often part of their routine.

Smooth news: Sleek-fitting leotards and bodysuits (*right*) were a requirement under these second-skin clothes to create a smooth silhouette.

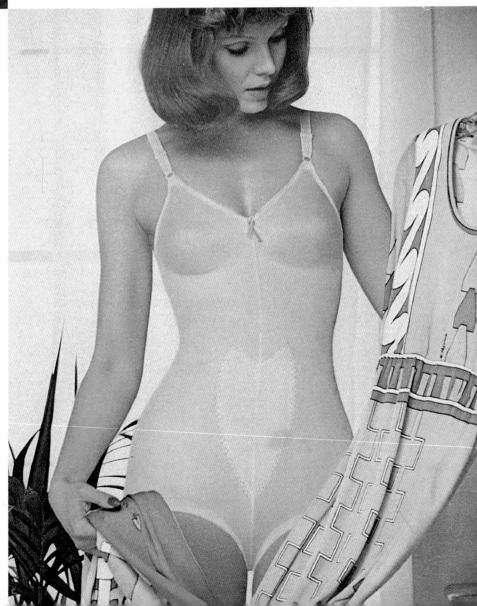

Swinging through the 1960s

The lighthearted, almost childlike approach to clothes of designers such as the influential Englishwoman Mary Quant meant that lingerie also grew simpler as the 1950s drew to a close, with briefer shapes, shorter lengths, and cutouts in sensual areas like the midriff.

By the mid decade, the new sportswear craze had hit town, and in 1965 Bert Stern photographed the model Marisa Berenson for American *Vogue* wearing a one-piece exercise suit by Rudi Gernreich. Inspired by a dancer's leotard and tights, her outfit appealed to both professional and social dancers, who were quick to recognize the advantages, and comfort, of such a suit. Its simplicity caught the mood of the times, while it also made the most of the latest in man-made fibers: Lycra.

Lycra was part of a new fiber group of elastomerics and elastanes that were three times as powerful as elastic, but far lighter. What was more, Lycra was resistant to abrasion, perspiration, and damage by detergents and lotions. As early as 1961, briefs made from fabrics such as nylon tricot were being given more support by minimal seaming and boning in Lycra.

Lycra was a natural for sportswear, for which there was an increasing demand. Tennis shorts had foreshadowed the revolution of sportswear as everyday wear, revealing parts of the body while still having a protective element that skirts lacked. Bra manufacturers were already at work on the first sports bras, which were designed to sustain the runner's movement while supporting the breasts. They provided ventilation and comfort without the hardware that irritated the skin.

Participation in expensive sports such as golf, polo, and yachting increased as people had more leisure time and more spending power. Purchasing sporting apparel for non-sporting activities became a sign of wealth and leisure, with après-ski clothing worn as often for visiting friends as for relaxing after a day on the slopes. By the mid 1970s, when materialism started to settle in and certain sportswear pieces became status symbols, both men and women, young or old, wore jogging suits and running shoes to the supermarket.

The birth of the fitness industry

The miniskirt of the 1960s had caused a turmoil in fashion by uncovering the legs, which had been concealed for centuries. In response came dancer-inspired leggings, footless tights, and leotards, which became the uniform of choice for many professional female athletes. The diminutive Russian gymnasts Olga Korbut and Nadia Comaneci were watched by the world as they performed stunning feats in skimpy leotards that bared their thighs in the early 1970s, for example. The leotard was a garment that was ideally suited to Lycra, and before long, Lycra leotards were widely available. Among the most highly sought were the varied shapes and cuts designed by Danskin, the famous dancewear company.

The concept was picked up by the fitness industry and the aerobics craze, led by American actress and fitness guru Jane Fonda, kept the leotard market in business. In the late 1970s, the British Pineapple dance studios, where Fonda's aerobics routines were taught and her video exercise tapes were created, brought leggings into the mass fashion market, and in 1979, Pineapple's founder and owner Debbie Moore developed her own line of garments based on ballet dress.

All that jazz: A 1960s one-piece exercise suit (*above*) gets jazzed up in a pink shade with white lace trim.

Peek-a-boo panties: Helen Gourlay exposes ruffled panties at the U.S. Open Tennis Championship in England in 1970.

Nudity: A trademark of its time

In the 1970s, for the first time in centuries, nudity became acceptable to the generally conservative American public. As interest and respect for other cultures and customs around the world increased, an acceptance of the human body in its natural state was seen through television programs and even at live sports events. Festivals and carnivals, the New Orleans Mardi Gras, and Las Vegas strip shows were all showcases for those who wanted to dress erotically, or minimally, in public, while the cheerleaders of the American football team the Dallas Cowboys made their debut in sexy shorts and vests. Even lingerie advertising campaigns designed for both print and television depicted the female body in its aesthetic sculptural form, with bras cut in lightweight, transparent fabrics showing off a woman's natural shape.

A real stretch: The Pineapple lingerie company turns out clothes that show off the body. A leopard patterned top and black stretch leggings (*left*) make the stretch in style.

Showing off: To highlight their sleek new bodies, women began wearing skimpy g-strings and cropped tops (*right*).

As the fitness craze boomed, every kind of exercise became fashionable. Body building grew in popularity for both men and women, the more fanatical sometimes using steroids to help them achieve their goal. In pursuit of the perfect body, women turned to plastic surgery to alter their natural shape, as well as following excessive diet and exercise regimes, often without considering the consequences. Changes were obvious in the male outline, too, as the bulky shape of American football players was widely adopted, with their exaggerated shoulders and padded thighs.

Keeping fit, exercise, and jogging all required new forms of apparel and had a significant effect on how people perceived their bodies. But other factors played a role as well. Waiflike models such as the 1960s and 1970s icon Twiggy made others strive for a slenderness that denoted sexual and financial independence, while the bikini entered mainstream swimwear after its introduction a decade before. Women began to search for something new, and came up with the skimpy G-string, a thin strand of string that was worn around the waist, covering practically nothing in front and revealing everything behind.

The body is born

The Paris fashion shows of the early 1970s exposed a wealth of skin, as did those in London and New York. Bare-breasted, leg-flashing models in chiffon wraps hid nothing, a sign of the times that saw breasts and bottoms on billboards and magazine covers all over the world. Attention was soon focused elsewhere, and the era of the body stocking was launched. Companies such as Dim, the French

Pump it up: A 1988 aerobics class (*above*) calls for flexible moves, made possible because of the latest collection of stretchy workout wear.

Rah! Rah! L.A. Rams cheerleaders (*above*) cheer on their team. But it's their new uniforms—cut in softer, more moveable fabrics—that score big points.

The secret's revealed: Victoria's Secret, the world-renowned, trend-setting lingerie company, slips into a season of swimsuits (*right*) with equally sexy tones.

pantyhose and lingerie makers, manufactured 40-denier stretch body stockings that fitted the body as closely as tights, while also shaping the breasts. Boasting thin elastic straps, they came in neutral colors such as natural, palma (pale caramel), earth, and black and created illusions of what the body looked like underneath. But although such body stockings were designed to appear sexy and create an image of desire, many women felt naked in them. They looked for comfort in the emerging popularity of maxi dresses and skirts, first worn by hippies, which hit the mainstream by 1975.

Fashion was swinging from one extreme to another, but despite the extra fabric of the newly lengthened apparel, the body was still being rediscovered. Long, flowing dresses represented protection, which meant undergarments could be eliminated. American companies began to specialize in provocative products which women could ogle in top-shelf magazines such as *Playboy* and *Lui* or on the motion-picture screens; they could order the erotic lingerie by mail order through specialty catalogs.

As morals changed, a lingerie trend emerged that embraced a wider sexuality; from pornographers and fetishists to voyeurs and sadomasochists. The company, Dim was a major contributor allowing its readers to feast their eyes on fantasy. Triumph was another player, their designs presented in soft photographic images. Advertisements for lingerie portrayed the erotic power of underwear, such as the campaign run by Aubade in France showing a man's hand on a scantily clad woman's body. As panty parties replaced Tupperware parties, the Miss Underwear 1983 contest, organized by the manager of a lingerie chain, tripled the chain's profits. In Tokyo, popular hangouts included bars where waitresses wore sexy underwear and touching was allowed.

Making the most of lightness

The 1974 invention of Spandex, another revolutionary man-made fiber, made lightweight body shapers possible for the first time. Most underwear was made of synthetic materials that lacked the luxurious feel of natural fibers. See-through lace no longer attempted to hide pubic hair with intricate patterns, body-caressing slips slit to the thigh and control panties with built-in roundness for flat bottoms were being purchased by women who felt sexually liberated but also wanted to feel seductive. In 1981, the French designer Pierre Cardin said, "New fashions have to shock the eyes in order to open them." And they did. Japanese designers such as Rei Kawakubo of Comme des Garçons and Yohji Yamamo challenged accepted ideas of femininity, disguising the shape of the body beneath layers of geometric, asymmetrical clothing. Such clothes were highly unglamorous but reflected the concern of women in the 1980s to please themselves with their clothes, rather than those who saw them. No longer did women rely on some distant arbitrator of taste and fashion; now, they bared or covered their bodies according to their own tastes, needs, and desires.

Athletic lingerie, designed by anatomical experts specializing in body stress, became all the rage during the 1980s; used both by sports enthusiasts and less active women. These gave support for women's bodies during the more strenuous sports activities, but the one-piece foundation, the leotard, bodysuit, and slim catsuit, were also widely worn by women in all walks of life. It was the American designer Azzedine Alaia who was largely responsible for bringing such garments to the public's attention, and by the time of the Autumn 1991/92 fashion shows, a number of designers were displaying them on the catwalks. Karl Lagerfeld featured long-sleeved, high-necked bodysuits in silver or bronze for day and evening, and Ozbek introduced catsuits with African tribal prints teamed with plain jackets and dresses. Donna Karan also presented catsuits, cut in stretch metallic and matte jersey and worn under sarongs, cape coats, and wraps, while *crêpe* was the signature material of Ghost, an English company owned by Tanya Sarne. Ghost added a new stretch chenille fabric to their 1991/92 collection.

Fabrics of the future

As the 1990s got underway, charity events such the Love Ball II (which raised money for AIDS research) were big in New York. These parties were packed with celebrities and cross-dressers, not to mention supermodels like Naomi Campbell and Linda Evangelista who also frequented London's Kinky Gerlinky nightclub. The retro scene of the 1960s and 1970s was revived, thanks to pop groups like Deee-Lite and De La Soul, who strutted about in Lycra and Spandex, stretch baby doll dresses, and tattoos, wearing wide headbands and false eyelashes.

Lycra/cotton and Lycra/nylon blends were still the fabrics of choice for young designers adding their own creations to the increasingly eclectic sportswear mix.

A set up: The Bjorn Borg challenger (*left*) orange matching tops and bottoms, blue/gray matching bra and knickers set (*top left*), and cropped top with pants make waves in 1997–98.

Sly cat: Karl Lagerfeld's catsuit (*right*) makes its mark as a sleek silhouette, showing off the body's sensual form.

The new sportswear changes the rules of the game: Here, a pair of 1987 Fila shorts get done up in sky blue with yellow and white piping.

Nothing clings like rubber

As a steady stream of man-made fabrics appeared, rubber came into fashion. Rubber designs from Nells Jorgensen, created by cutting and draping rubber and utilizing its stretching and clinging qualities, opened many new design doors and showed off even more of the female body, while American designer Azzedine Alaia, known as the King of Cling, invented a new shape for the mini in 1987. He combined wool jersey with Latex for a second-skin look. His close-fitting line of body-conscious stretch garments, including leggings and micro-minis, called attention to women on New York City streets who walked about town tugging on their forever shortening hemlines, but created a sense of sexuality and chic among those who wore them.

Gordon Henderson, described in *Women's Wear Daily* as the great synthesizer of body clinging sportswear, Ozbek and other British designers mixed stretch Lycra sports and exercise fabrics with exotic cotton and silk prints from India and Africa, producing a look that combined freedom of movement with glamor. The American designer Isaac Mizrahi promoted his kind of hybrid ethnicity. "I want my clothing to be as comfortable as a pair of pajamas... but suitable for Wall Street," he said, "and I want them to be very American in feeling." Active sportswear was taken to the next level with the introduction of new fabrics such as Microfiber, Thinsulate, and Polartec, which were increasingly used in outdoor wear. They provided warmth without bulk, creating a toasty, streamlined effect.

As models once again flaunted their stick thin boyish bodies with an elegant edge, see-through mesh net shirts and dresses worn braless to show off healthy, firmly toned bodies underneath turned up in and out of clubs. Less fabric was used in many designs, perhaps in response to the financial recession of the 1990s, and cotton became the essential fabric in bodywear and streetwear. The camisole leotard with a low racing back appeared, worn with Capri tights from Marika Fitness Apparel, and the record-holding American sprinter Christine Farmer-Patrick made fashion and athletic headlines by wearing a cropped top and cycle shorts in a brightly colored, nylon/Lycra blend on the track.

It seemed that sportswomen still had the power to change fashions, and to shock, almost a century after the French tennis player Suzanne Lenglen startled the crowds at Wimbledon in the early 1920s. But what had seemed shocking then was nothing in comparison to the skintight, minimalist, Lycra-based sportswear of the late 1990s. Immobilizing underclothes had gone, replaced by body-clinging lingerie pieces that were as suited to swimming, jogging, tennis, and golf as they were to scuba diving and hang gliding. The sporting revolution was complete.

Up to speed: Florence Griffith Joyner, otherwise known as FloJo, shows off the latest sportswear (*right*) at the 1987 World Athletics Championship in Rome.

Wolford

Wolford, an Austrian company founded in 1949, is among the foremost innovators of women's hosiery and bodywear. Its international trendsetting image is at the core of the fifty-year-old company's philosophy, which strives to unite beauty, femininity, and modernity with a touch of the exotic.

Soon after World War II drew to a close, and just a decade after the American firm DuPont introduced the first nylon stockings, Wolford was founded by two farsighted businessmen, Walter Palmers and Reinhold Wolff. The company was based in the small town of Bregenz, situated between Lake Constance and the Austrian mountains.

After World War II, nylon stockings were in great demand, and initially Wolford produced hosiery to fulfill contracts for a range of different companies. The company was often at the forefront of hosiery developments, combining trend-setting innovation with technological advances and comprehensive quality control. It experimented with the new bicomponent yarn Cantrece as early as 1969 and introduced the first products to incorporate such yarn in 1971 when it launched its "Perfection" line of hosiery.

This experimentation with new fibers continued, resulting in 1976 with Touchlon, a synthetic material much like silk. During the 1980s, Wolford improved its silky feeling hosiery, introducing its famous "Satin Touch" in 1986, and "Opaque de Luxe" legwear of 1987. These featured satin sheens and silky luster, and included Lycra.

After Wolford was floated on the stock market in 1988, the company began to establish its own brand name. Before long, it had created a reputation for exclusive hosiery and bodywear, and extended its range to include swimwear as well.

Wolford was noted for its dedication to quality. As much as fifteen percent of manufacturing time is devoted to quality assurance, and at each phase of a garment's manufacture, detailed control procedures record the production steps, from seams and mesh structure to color, size, and touch.

The body beautiful

It was during the decade of the 1980s that Wolford introduced its first collection of bodies. The earliest, made of lace, were inspired by the success of a 1981 range of legwear made of the finest delicate lace. Six years later, in 1987, lace bodies made their first appearance, with Wolford applying its hosiery expertise to bodywear. "Bodies without side seams" appeared in 1992, and within just five more years, seamfree second-skin bodies, introduced as "Swimbodies" in 1997, created the perfect figure-hugging fit for women of all shapes and sizes.

Computer technology had a dramatic impact upon hosiery design, as with other areas, and was happily embraced by Wolford. The company's sophisticated computer technology created vast numbers of pattern possibilities, which were combined

Kicking up a storm: Sheer hosiery from Wolford gives women something to click their heels about (right). Some could even be heard saying: "There's no hosiery like Wolford's, there's no hosiery like Wolford's."

Second skin stuff: With underclothes like this velvety soft pair of thigh-highs (*above*), who needs to wear anything else. The matte fabric and striped band give it a sophisticated touch.

Sporty turns sexy: This sleek and sophisticated bodysuit (*right*) boasts cutting-edge style, thanks to a slick shape and piping trim.

with new yarns and high-tech knitting machines to produce branded products of exquisite beauty and the highest quality. By the 1990s, Wolford was mentioned in the same breath as the best-known international designers, showing that the company had established itself as a top producer in the international luxury market.

The company divided its leg and bodywear into separate fashion groups and offered four fashion seasons every year, in accordance with the mainstream fashion industry. Its inquisitive,

experimental creative team worked in partnership with top designers, attending all the seasonal collections in order to forecast colors and trends. As a result, Wolford's fashionable styles were chosen by many of the world's international designers, such as Vivienne Westwood, Alexander MacQueen, Katherine Hamnett, Coco Chanel, Ungaro, Christian Lacroix, Dolce & Gabbana, Romeo Gigli, Laura Biagiotti, and Helmut Lang, to complement their collections on the catwalk and in their advertising.

By the late 1990s, the Wolford name appeared independently in more than 190 boutiques in exclusive shopping areas across the world. Some were joint venture partnerships with independent franchisers, while others acted as shops within shops, but all provided a branded identity and ambiance for the entire Wolford collection.

Pineapple

It was in a former fruit warehouse in London's Covent Garden that Pineapple was founded by Debbie Moore in 1979. In less than three years, she transformed a rundown building into the most famous dance studio in the world, launched a collection of body-conscious clothing that was to revolutionize fashion, and, in 1982, floated her company on the London Stock Exchange.

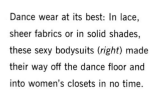

O ver the next two decades, Debbie Moore was twice nominated as the Veuve Cliquot Business Woman of the Year—quite an achievement for a former model who left school aged fifteen with almost no qualifications.

The history of the dance studio, the clothing collection, and its famous entrepreneur are inseparable. Pineapple started from modest beginnings. When the dance studio where Debbie Moore regularly worked out closed down in 1978, she invested her savings in a large premises which had been used to store pineapples. Her plan was to turn it

into studios where London's dance community could enjoy a range of classes, from modern dance, jazz, and ballet to tap, all under one roof. Pineapple's relaxed, friendly atmosphere broke down the elitist barriers that often surrounded the dance world, and before long, young women working in local offices were also attending the dance classes as the trend for fitness grew.

Debbie Moore recognized Lycra's versatility—it was easy to care for, crease resistant, needed no ironing, and retained its original shape—and as the fitness craze gathered pace, so demand increased for comfortable, fashionable dancewear. In response, Moore designed a collection of dancewear made from the new Lycra, and manufactured it under the Pineapple clothing label. Among the most original of these was the "body," an item which derived from the dancer's leotard and which went on to become one of the staple items of 1990s underwear. "Much of what I do is inspired by the stretchy clothing of dancers," Moore has said. "I started

Lingerie leader: The brainchild behind the Pineapple lingerie line, Debbie Moore (*above*) based her collection on dance-inspired clothes. The result: Sleek, streamlined leotards and bodysuits that every woman could wear.

Dance wear at its best: In lace, sheer fabrics or in solid shades, these sexy bodysuits (*right*) made their way off the dance floor and into women's closets in no time.

designing originally because I couldn't find a body in the right color or style."

Lycra's unique corseting effect helped to shape even the least shapely of bodies and combined flexibility with comfort. Before long, her body-conscious clothing was making a fashion statement, not only in the studio but also on the streets. Pineapple leotards, swimsuits, bodies, hold-up stockings, boned bras, leggings, catsuits, dresses, sweatshirts, and T-shirts could be bought either from fashionable Pineapple shops or from its franchises in upscale London department stores such as Harrods and Miss Selfridge. A thriving mail-order business provided clothes to those who lived outside London and other major cities.

Such rapid and unforeseen expansion was bound to have a price, especially as by 1986 Pineapple had also purchased expensive studios on New York's Broadway, and created a wholesale clothing operation. It had also become part of the Prospect Group following its 1982 stock market flotation, one of seven companies that made up the whole. When the Prospect Group talked of disposing of Pineapple after heavy losses between 1986 and 1987, Debbie Moore headed a management buy-out of her company. In March 1988, she reprivatized her company, buying back her name, the studios, the fashion line, and debts of £500,000 for just £1.

By autumn of 1988, Moore had given all the centers a facelift, built a new management team—a mixture of old and new faces—and injected a great feeling of renewed energy into the Pineapple business. Just one year later, with a revitalized company image, Debbie Moore at Pineapple was nominated for "Contemporary Designer of the Year" at the British Fashion Awards. This remarkable comeback was followed up by repeated nominations for the British Fashion Council's "More Dash Than Cash" awards, for four consecutive years from 1990 to 1993.

With Pineapple back under her direct control, Moore continued to do what she did best—running a chain of successful dance studios and designing contemporary dancewear. But her flair and imagination continued to show itself in new lines, including Pineapple cosmetics made from homeopathic ingredients. Their brand name "Survival of the Fittest"—epitomized Moore's approach to life.

Black or white: Demi bras and bikini bottoms (*below*) get the transparent treatment when cut in sheer fabrics that add interest and intrigue.

6

Girdles and Garters

Although the playwright William Shakespeare mentioned the original concept of a girdle, or belt, in his famous comedy *A Midsummer Night's Dream*, written in 1594—"I'll put a girdle round about the Earth in forty minutes," he wrote—it was not until the 1920s that the modern girdle became an item of fashion. Lingerie designers introduced them as an alternative to the dreaded corset. Garter belts were an independent way to suspend stockings. But despite its constricting nature—a feature that led to its virtual demise in the 1960s—the fitness craze that swept the world from the 1970s onward led to a slight resurgence of the girdle, albeit in modern-day forms and fabrics. It was not until the late 1990s, however, that foundation garments such as the girdle were definitely back in fashion, such as waist-clinching briefs and panties, control briefs, and briefs designed specifically to slim and shape when wearing trousers. Women's bodies became packaged in a specialized way—from garments designed to taper stomach muscles, hips and thighs, to stretch shorts with side panels to compress thunder thighs.

Really racy: A skirt caught in the wind (*above*) reveals stockings and garters which were typically worn underneath.

The perfect uniform: Mary Quant's black matching bra, knickers, garter belt and stockings (*right*).

You're suspended! These original pairs of suspenders (*above*), introduced in the 1880s, were meant to hold women's underclothes in place. They offered plenty of support and later even added style.

CONTROL AS THE GOAL

Suspenders (also known as garters) in the 1880s originally "suspended" a woman's underclothes. In many instances, they were no more than a band of ribbon, meant to support stockings. A woman who could afford them would dress in a chemise and drawers, a corset with garters, or suspenders—then known as the basque-black stockings—a camisole, and one or two petticoats were her staple accessories.

By the 1920s, however, the arrival of man-made fibres such as rayon and artifical silk altered the job of the garter belt, as well as that of roll-on stockings and the teddy. Within a decade, the short-lived vogue of the garter belt had come to an end as women began to roll their stockings around their garters above the knees.

Protectors of virtue

The earliest girdle known of in the West was the chastity belt, or girdle. This was widely used in the Middle East to ensure the chastity of women by enclosing the female genitals with a secure structure, and was encountered by the medieval Crusaders who left Europe to fight a Holy War against the Islamic world from the 1200s onward.

Returning Crusaders brought the idea of the chastity belt back with them to Europe. Most such girdles were made of a broad band of material or metal that encircled the loins and thighs, with a necessary opening where the material or metal passed between the legs. The material or metal was attached to a hip band which could be adjusted as required and made secure with a locking device at the sides, front or back. There were many different types of chastity belt, some heavy and substantial, others a simple one-piece girdle and yet another in two pieces, to give protection both in front and behind. In some cases, chastity girdles took the form of a grille, which was suspended and supported by chains which hung from a hip band.

Such an uncomfortable and restrictive garment was not tolerated for long by women, however, and soon passed out of fashion. Thereafter, the girdle dropped out of sight until the invention of elasticated fabrics in the early 1900s. By the 1920s, older women still relied on lace-up corsets, but the younger generation turned to girdles and belts to keep their figures trim. The new light, unrestrictive foundation garments were made with woven elastic, and were incorporated at first into low-backed corsets with up-lift brassières. These were cut long enough to grip hips and thighs tightly but were often uncomfortable to wear.

Nonetheless, the idea of the roll-on corset, the early prototype of the girdle, continued to gain in popularity even though a few kinks in these new lingerie pieces needed to be ironed out. By the 1930s, for example, Warner Brothers had launched a two-way stretch corset called La Gant, which was made of latex. Its success was marred by the fact that this new roll-on fabric rode up as it was worn, and so had to be developed further.

The distinction between linen and structural underwear became increasingly defined. Early lingerie in fine cotton and silk, "linen," was worn next to the skin as a covering for the naked body, used both as a temperature moderator for keeping the body

The girdle's got it: Offering support, shape and a feminine edge, the girdle (*left*) made its comeback in the 1920s as women relied on it to give them the sleeker, slimmer shapes they wouldn't be able to otherwise achieve.

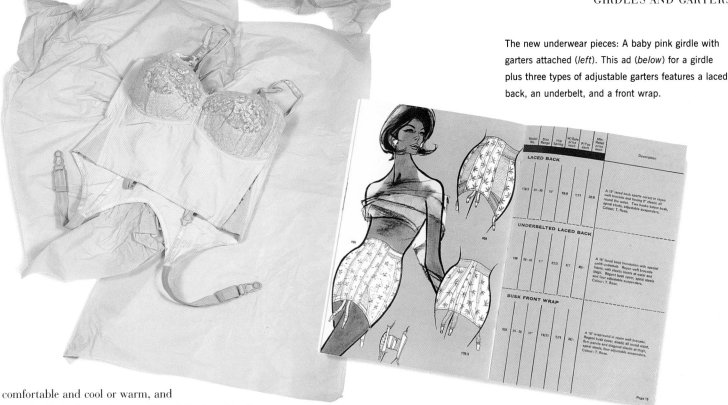

The new underwear pieces: A baby pink girdle with garters attached (*left*). This ad (*below*) for a girdle plus three types of adjustable garters features a laced back, an underbelt, and a front wrap.

comfortable and cool or warm, and as a hygienic layer that would shield the skin from discomfort. On the other hand, structural garments made from the new elasticized fabrics either restricted or enlarged natural contours, providing basic feminine shapes.

As the market for the girdle developed in the 1940s and 1950s, it was seen in many different cuts, fabrics, and shapes. Berlei, Gossard and Silhouette made utility bras and girdles in the 1940s, which was also the decade of the popular Scandale girdle. In the years that followed the end of World War II, women could choose from a variety of foundation garments, including the pantie-corselette and pantie-girdle, to obtain the right combination of cover and control.

In 1945, for example, fashion editors advised readers to buy the new pantie-girdle with built-in padding that would emphasize their buttocks, although the role of the girdle was still being questioned. One commentator described it as a queer pink undergarment of what appeared to be a strong thick elastic material, with 4-5 inches (10-12 cm) suspenders attached to grip the tops of stockings.

Even so, the girdle took over the job of control for most women after 1950 or so. Whether elasticized, side-hooked, or bust fronted, it remained a firm favorite. Aertex underwear and corsetry was prominent in the 1950s, advertised with stockings and garter belts, as finer cottons became popular. Their smoother, more lightweight, and obviously more expensive qualities eventually lost out to cheaper artificial fibers such as nylon and polyester, however. (These went on to dominate the girdle market right up to the early 1970s under the trademark Terylene.)

Stylish nylon

Nylon came in many forms. There was machine knit nylon tafetta, nylon net, nylon marquisette, voile lace nylon seersucker (as used by the Adlis Bra Company in 1955), and nylon lace (seen in the English Rose collection of bras and girdles, launched in Spring 1955.) The Little X stretch corset, advertised in 1956, made waves when it ran with an African-American model in a black leotard wearing a white bra and girdle. Revolutionary for the times, dark models were then used for light clothes and vice versa. By the mid 1950s, girdles were seen everywhere, but women still puzzled over what to call them. Such restrictive bodyshaping pieces were often referred to by their brand names rather than by the terms "girdle" or "roll-on."

As the 1960s approached, girdles became increasingly decorative. One model from Warner that went on sale in 1957 had flowers embroidered on the front panels, while others were decorated with gold threads, colored rhinestones, and diamanté stars. Mixed fiber underwear incorporating wool, nylon, combed cotton, and nylon, orlon, banlon, and other mixtures was in production by 1958, most

French fashions rule

Suspenders, used by women to hold up stockings, were first seen in Britain with the 1876 arrival of the French spectacle, the Grand Opera Bouffe. The company presented a show in Leicester Square, and the public was much struck by the French dancers whose stockings were held in place over naked thighs with suspenders. A belt with suspenders attached was introduced in 1887, designed to be worn over the corset, and was being widely worn by the 1890s. The first suspender attached to the corset itself appeared in 1901.

Just your size: These girdles (*right*) come with adjustable garters so you can adjust the fit to suit your individual body type.

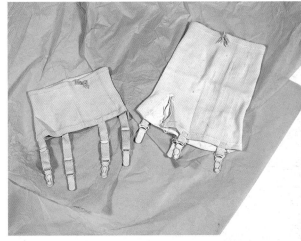

Freedom of movement: Girdles and garters (*right*) may look cumbersome to lingerie wearers today but in the middle of the twentieth century they instilled women with a new confidence in their bodies and represented a whole new freedom of movement. The matching bras helped too; this set by Chantelle.

Chantelle

What a waist! Not only did girdles (*below*) give the entire body a slimmer look, but some featured exaggerated waistlines that created a sexy hourglass look. This high contraband is reinforced with elura tummy-flattening bands.

with attached suspenders, at least after pantyhose and tights were created in the 1960s. Coordinated bras and girdles were increasingly popular, most fairly subdued in color and fabric, as the roll-on of two-way stretch elastic gained ground throughout the 1960s and into the 1970s, providing extra control without extra weight.

But despite their pleasant aesthetic appearance, early versions made of rubber or latex only stretched horizontally, so women constantly tugged to keep them in place. Spandex girdles of the 1960s were much lighter than their predecessors and could shave 2 inches (5 cm) off the body but left painful welts on the skin. "You scratched yourself for a half hour after taking your girdle off," says Audrey Smaltz, an early girdle model for Lane Bryant. Such inconveniences encouraged women of the late 1960s in their crusade against wearing any such types of restrictive underwear, but the innovation of tights and pantyhose soon made roll-on girdles unnecessary for holding up stockings.

The return of the waist

The year 1969 introduced a new type of girdle. The soft cup bandeau and girdle, a plunging girdle with a reinforced stomach panel and rubber grip bottom behind stretch lace, was created by Lady Marlene. Pantyhose with an incorporated panty girdle, to be used without garters, were developed by Denver in both nude and, most in demand, black. Panty girdles with lacy cuffs and stay-in-place bands saved women the trouble of layering unnecessary undergarments over their underclothes.

The return of the waist in the early 1970s ensured the continuing popularity of the girdle. Those in printed floral patterns, seen on other lingerie, too, were produced by leading lingerie manufacturers. The Berlei catalog of 1971 advertised new fabrics, for example, and the American brand Playtex introduced the famous Cross Your Heart Bra and Living Girdle. Women generally wanted one of two foundation garments: either something powerful just below the waist, or a light smoothing garment from the bust down to their thighs.

With the onset of the fitness-conscious years, the popularity of the girdle was threatened by the introduction of figure-control panties. Suddenly it was models such as the tummy-control slacks liner,

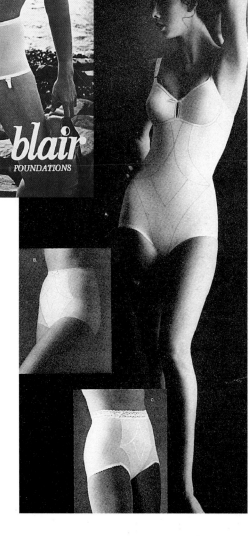

Move over Bond girls: This Blair ad featuring three girls in girdles and garters (*left*) on secret assignment from Sweden reveals their undercover weapons.

introduced by Tru Balase, that brought women back to lingerie departments. These had a built-in brief and were made of 86% nylon and 14% Lycra Spandex. A high-waist control brief from Flexels, with reinforced hip front and back panels and a tricot-lined snap crotch, made the fashion forecast. Popular body-smoothing shapes that offered easy action and comfort included an Antron III and Lycra brief with a rear shaped panel by Youth Craft/Charmfit, and briefs trimmed in stretch nylon lace with a support panel from Vanity Foundations.

The high-waister by Deluxe Fashions featured an all-around high top of Helenca elastic on an Antron (DuPont) nylon body with decorative front stitching and a stretch brief with a reinforced front panel. Pastel colors like white, lemon, pink, blue, and jade showed up from Lily of France, in addition to black and beige, and Bali created bare briefs set with double-layered front panels and shirred lace bands at the legs. Light control briefs with two support panels and rubber hose grippers, in nylon and Lycra Spandex, were developed by Kayser, while the molded brief was Vassarette's contribution. Its long leg girdles and panty liner hipsters cut in lace sold under the name "Second Glance."

Looking to the future

By the mid 1970s, women who were dieting and needed help, or who needed control but didn't want to be strapped into old-fashioned heavy elastic, could turn to the comfortable It's A Cinch all-in-one all-over control panty brief that covered the torso. Seamless cups and molded cup versions in Antron III nylon and Lycra Spandex were both available and sold out when they hit retail stores in the mid 1970s.

Every designer had its creation in the panty-brief market. Stores stocked Adler's Skinny Waist series, Lady Marlene's Deep Plunge Body Briefer, Gossard's Slim-ees in a moderate control weight of Antron nylon and Lycra spandex, and Sears showed Olga's Wunder Pantsliner to wear under slacks. In an effort to compromise between an overly constricting girdle and ordinary non-support panties, Vassarette's Pant-suasion debuted in November 1972. Other controlling options included Jantzen's Jungle Blossom brief, Maidenform's All the Time control panty, and Warner's Tom-Boy lightweight control brief. Lingerie grew even more smooth and supple for Fall 1974.

The roll-on industry witnessed a decline in sales that worried manufacturers, as a DuPont study in the mid 1970s showed that women disliked the restriction of girdles. Some believed they caused physical problems, such as flabby muscles and varicose veins. In an attempt to woo women back, "the girdle that loses as you do" was introduced in 1976, made of memory-stretch Lycra Spandex and nylon. These components allowed the garment to adjust to a woman's figure as she changed in size.

Toward the end of the 1970s, health concerns prompted the introduction and widespread adoption of cotton gussets, as

Girdles of every girth: No matter what your body type, these girdles (*above*) are for you. Check them out in these different shapes and sizes.

Girdles make a fashion statement: No longer just for functional purposes, girdles, garters and bras all team up to create a fashionable set (*far left*).

Great to spy on...or in: Agent Provocateur's matching black bra with girdle and garters (*above*) add a little mystery to a woman's ensemble.

Don't get cross: It may be a little tight but the cross-laced panel on the front of this girdle (*right*) adds a decorative effect. Covering the area from waist to upper thigh, it offers comprehensive control.

The girdle revolution: In the 1990s, new technology allowed designers to create bodysuits and swimsuits (*below*) that served the girdle purpose.

opposed to gussets made of non-absorbent nylon. Cotton returned in full force, especially when combined with polyester, and went on to reclaim the status it had had at the start of the century as an underwear fabric staple. Modern technological developments meant there was something for everyone on offer, including the late 1970s molded pantie girdle which was strong but almost invisible as well as comfortable to wear and easy to wash. The word "girdle" was practically extinct by 1978, however, replaced by the less old-fashioned "control garments." Spandex, cotton, and wool blends coupled with petroleum-based Spandex, took center stage in designer lines from the likes of Alaia and Kamali, and these stretch garments became increasingly comfortable through the 1980s.

The modern girdle

The changes in attitude and lifestyle that accompanied the onset of the 1980s continued to make the girdle obsolete. "My gynecologist told me to diet and exercise, and never to wear a girdle again," one woman told her friends. For many, it seemed like cheating to wear a body-shaping garment, although women often did not want to admit they were out of shape or growing old. "The girdle conjures up the kind of clothes that looked bulky and lumpy," said one anti-girdleite. "It's uncomfortable, restrictive and old-fashioned." For those who did believe that a little re-shaping never hurt anyone, designer Lady Marlene created the high waist panty girdle of 100% Lycra Spandex in 1982, complete with reinforced tummy panel and rubberized hose grippers.

It was the same conforming Lycra Spandex fabric that brought the girdle into the 1990s, a decade during which see-through slips were worn as dresses and women strived for coke-bottle figures by wearing rubber girdles and pointed bras even when they were vaccuuming the house. Celebrity singer/entertainer Madonna promoted corsetry with suspender belts throughout the decade, and her

plethora of fans followed her lead, wearing form-shaping underwear as outerwear... everywhere.

By the end of the 1990s, the introduction of looser fashions had helped to make the gripping girdle all but disappear, although other body-shaping pieces had replaced it. At the Town Shop, a lingerie boutique on Manhattan's exclusive Upper West Side, stretch slips and Slim Suits, the bathing suit guaranteed to take 1 inch (2.5 cm) off every woman's body, were sold with a free tape measure. The last word in twentieth-century girdles were half-slips with panties sewn in, such as the Hip Slip and Under Wonder, which sold at New York's Bloomingale's and other exclusive department stores around the world.

Taking a cue from the bra, girdles and their imposters became more specialized at packaging women's bodies. There were different garments to taper stomach muscles, hips and thighs, from stretch shorts with side panels to compress thunder thighs, and panties with front panels that flatten tummies but not buttocks. These panties were designed by American Carol Green who said, "After two kids, I still looked good in clothes until I turned sideways."

By the late 1990s, foundation garments such as girdles and bras were definitely back in fashion. After all, the fashionable, body-hugging Spandex dress of the late decade was unforgiving to women of a certain age. By 1996, shapewear, originally inspired by the Wonderbra of the 1980s, was on offer in all forms, including the waist-cinching briefs by Sara Lee in white, matte and shine. Control briefs such as Secret Shapers by Olga caught on, seen at their most radical in control cycling pants of nylon and Lycra from the Body Slimmers collection by Nancy Ganz at Warnaco.

Girdles for men, and other support articles, were also big sellers, used to give support for hernias or back trouble, to hide love handles or to camouflage a couple of extra pounds to fit into a tuxedo for a special occasion. The physical fitness craze was a boon for the girdle, whose old-fashioned associations would have seen its demise without the late-twentieth century fad for toned bodies.

Not all women returned to the girdle, however. Helen Gurley Brown, a former editor of the woman's magazine *Cosmopolitan*, admitted that although she applauded other women for trying to fix their bodies with a girdle, she would not be wearing one herself. "You crush yourself in a girdle and literally take three inches off but it goes right to your rib cage." Earlier women had less choice in the matter. As the actress Eva Gabor once said, "Women must suffer for everything. Since when have you been comfortable in an evening gown? You can't be comfortable if you want to look smashing. Any honest woman will tell you that."

Dolce & Gabbana

A chance introduction in Milan between a young Sicilian, Domenico Dolce, whose family ran a small clothing business, and a graduate from art school, a Milanese with Venetian background, Stefano Gabbana, was to result in one of the most dynamic fashion partnerships of the 1980s and 1990s.

When Dolce & Gabbana joined forces in the early 1980s, they pooled a wealth of talent and knowledge. Dolce had grown up in the rag trade, as his family ran a small clothing business. Combined with Gabbana's art school training, this knowledge of fabric led to a design style that was both romantic and voluptuous. It drew inspiration from the passionate personality of southern Italians, as epitomized by the screen goddesses Sophia Loren and Anna Magnani.

Dolce & Gabbana's meteoric rise to fame started in 1985, when they were invited to participate in the October Milan Fashion Collections. They were selected to represent the best new talent in Italian fashion, and succeeded admirably, quickly attracting the attention of the world's fashion press. Dolce & Gabbana's annual fashion show became a mandatory appointment, and within two years, in 1987, Dolce & Gabbana had opened a showroom in via Santa Cecilia in Milan.

Soon afterward, they combined forces with Dolce Saverio, the clothing firm owned by Domenico Dolce's family, to produce women's outerwear. Their signature corset dress and pinstripe suits, neatly summarized by *Harper's Bazaar* magazine in 1996 as "sexy alla Italiana boudoir-for-the-boardroom fashion," hit a nerve with confident, liberated women of the late 1990s.

Dolce & Gabbana's clothing style celebrated women as they truly are, reveling in their hips and breasts. The style recalls the Italian tradition and Mediterranean roots that the designers feel. They take Sicily and the women of the south as the underlying theme of their collections. She is a woman who has a strong personality; is passionate; but a woman who is not afraid to show her femininity. The elements that are always present and that have become the Dolce & Gabbana signature are the corset and the bra, "enveloping women's breasts like a shrine, because the breast is the most important element in a woman. It stands for her maternity, eroticism and femininity." In the collections, it is always there, combined with those *guêpieres* (such as the one

that Cindy Crawford wore when she opened the Spring/Summer 1992 fashion show), and those panties that are mainly black, but can also be in nude, white, gray, or brown, in leopard and flower print, or even pinstriped, and in elastic, lace, satin, or stretch fabric. The manufacturing technique for lingerie, such as the use of whalebones, combined with the Italian tradition of tailoring, have also influenced the construction of Dolce & Gabbana's dresses—with bras underneath and the bra straps visible.

The concept of underwear as outer wear is definitely a constant theme of their collections; with designs being snapped up by celebrities from Madonna to film star Isabella Rossellini.

Such was the demand for their clothes that they expanded again, turning to menswear, perfume, bath products, eyewear, home accessories, and even music, among other areas. By the time Dolce & Gabbana opened their New York showroom in 1990, they had launched both lingerie and beachwear, introduced a men's collection, and entered the Japanese market.

The company had soon won a host of awards for its menswear collection, perfumes, and packaging. Indeed, Dolce & Gabbana's Pour Homme received an unprecedented accolade when it was awarded the French Oscar des Parfums in 1995, the first time this award had been presented to an Italian fragrance.

In 1996, the company celebrated its tenth anniversary with the publication of *Ten Years of Dolce & Gabbana*, a collection of its most significant advertising and editorial images. Such a departure from the catwalk summed up the company's attitude toward itself and the service it offered its customers: It was not just a collection of clothing and accessories, but an attitude and a lifestyle in which passion triumphs.

Dangerous curves ahead: Dolce & Gabbana celebrate the female form (*left*) with form-fitting silhouettes paired with working-women's shirts and ties that scream independence and power.

Flora Nikrooz

Flora Nikrooz negligées are a combination of feminine fantasy and floating form. As the business she established with her husband in the 1970s became a multimillion dollar, multinational enterprise, Nikrooz stuck to her original aim—to bring out a woman's inherent flirtatious femininity using pleats, delicate beading, and lace.

Born in Iran, Flora Nikrooz had trained as a jewelry designer before she moved to New York. Once there, she turned her design training to good use, employing it as she sketched out her first tentative lingerie fashions. Her talent gained immediate recognition from underwear manufacturers, and before long, her creative designs were featured in the windows of New York's leading department stores.

Her meeting with, and subsequent marriage to, the American Marvin Backer in the 1970s profoundly influenced her career, and subsequent designs. His business experience in the sale and merchandising of lingerie inspired her to create beautiful garments with a painstaking attention to detail. The husband and wife team were an ideal business partnership, with Nikrooz designing a small collection of lingerie, and Marvin selling the designs to New York department stores. Their first order sold out within two days.

Nikrooz's designs were identified by their perfect pleating, delicate beading, and lacy bodices, and her feel for popular taste was confirmed when her Frou Frou negligée appeared on the cover of the Victoria's Secret mail order catalog. The item broke all previous lingerie sales records, selling approximately 3,000 pieces within weeks and ensuring that thereafter, her lingerie was stocked in leading

What's right for night? Flora Nikrooz knows best with her seductive silhouettes (*above*) that enlighten even the most sober evening—here, she flirts with fashion and fun in one.

department stores and boutiques across the whole of the United States.

By the late 1990s, Flora Nikrooz was creating five collections a year, for Spring, Summer, Resort, Fall, and Winter, each of which consisted of anything from between 50 and 120 lingerie pieces. These conformed to the guiding principle which had inspired her to take up lingerie design some twenty-five years earlier: "No matter how far we've come, women still spend most of their hours in a man's world, conforming to the rules mandated by that society. Lingerie helps a woman find that special place that belongs only to a woman. My designs bring out the flirtatious femininity that is Woman at her finest."

The power of pleats: Strong and defined yet soft and sensual accents make Flora Nikrooz designs (*left*) fit for fantasy—she shimmies her way into every woman's evening wardrobe with style.

Smooth sailing: Frederick Mellinger gave the bust a boost with this seamless push-up number (*left*), which became the perfect foil for the tightest tee.

Glitz and glamor: The Frederick's of Hollywood storefront (*right*) and its sultry selections gave stars of the silver screen a sophisticated Vegas-inspired edge.

Frederick's of Hollywood

When Frederick Mellinger began his mail order operation for lingerie in 1946, operating out of a tiny loft in Manhattan, New York, as "Frederick's of Fifth Avenue," it is doubtful he anticipated that fifty years later, his company would own over two hundred stores throughout the United States of America, as well as distributing over fifty million mail order catalogs a year.

In 1946, when nice American girls wore white cotton "bloomers," Frederick Mellinger caused a sensation with his sexy, black panties, bras, nightgowns, and peignoirs. During his stint as a GI during World War II, Mellinger had done extensive research, questioning fellow soldiers about their idea of a perfect woman and her underwear. By the time he left the army and went into business, he had

settled on his winning formula: "The company designs each undergarment, whether it is a baby-doll nightgown or push-up bra, to make a woman more alluring to a man and more attractive to herself when she looks in the mirror."

A year later, Mellinger moved his company to Hollywood, and renamed it Frederick's of Hollywood. His sensuous lingerie was an immediate hit with Hollywood's film stars, chiming as it did

with the glamorous image of the film studios and Hollywood lifestyle. Mellinger owed his success to understanding women and fashion, and kept his eye on style trends. His "Hollywood Profile" of the 1950s, for example, was inspired by film costume designers of the time, and fashion-conscious women sought out his company's pointed, circle-stitched bras sold under brand names such as Missiles and Snow Cones.

Mellinger had a gift for publicity—"All women are not created equal," said Mellinger. "No matter how beautiful the outer garment, without the right foundation, the look will be wrong." His company introduced a continuous stream of new, innovative products, from the first padded bra in 1947 to 1948's "Rising Star," the world's first push-up bra. In the 1960s came the innovatory "Cadillac" bra, the company's bestseller. It was reputed to change the wearer so much that "you came in looking like a Chevy and left looking like a Cadillac," according to Mellinger. The front-hook bra was first designed by Frederick of Hollywood's, as were bras with shoulder pads, padded girdles, and body shapers. There was even the "Mood Stone Panty" which changed color with the wearer's change of mood, and musical panties, introduced in 1984, which could provide a tune for every occasion from The Wedding March to Happy Birthday.

In the 1950s, Mellinger dared to advertise his lingerie in both men's and women's magazines, a marketing strategy which paid off handsomely. By the 1970s, when women protesting against excessive and repressive underwear picketed Frederick's flagship store in Hollywood, Mellinger had enough media nous to pronounce in public that the "law of gravity will win out." It was excellent publicity, and sales of his bras soared across the continent.

Mellinger had a knack of picking future celebrities to work as models in Frederick's of Hollywood's catalogs, posters, advertisements, and fashion shows (the actresses Pamela Anderson Lee and Traci Bingham appeared in his lingerie catalogs, and later landed roles in the television series *Baywatch*) but by the early 1980s, he had recognized the danger in Frederick's of Hollywood associating itself too blatantly with overtly sexy lingerie. America's more conservative women wanted good quality mainstream lingerie which was soft and sensual, but definitely not sleazy; the company adjusted its marketing accordingly.

By the late 1990s, Frederick's was massively successful, with more than 80,000 visitors a year visiting the world's first Lingerie Museum, opened by the company in 1989. It features garments worn by Hollywood's stars over the last fifty years, from Ava Gardner's pantaloons to Madonna's bustier. When thieves broke into the museum in 1992, stealing garments such as Katy Sagal's bra, ten people tried to claim the reward by presenting copies of the original.

Despite changing fashions, Frederick's of Hollywood has kept apace with the look of the day while sticking to its founder's original determination to satisfy women's desire for sensual and soft lingerie. Frederick Mellinger retired in 1984, and died in 1990, but his company was set to provide the lingerie market with original and ground-breaking garments to the end of the century and beyond the year 2000.

Bustier babes: A cone-shaped bra, thick seams and gold fabric (*below*) put Frederick's of Hollywood on the seduction map.

7

Stockings and Pantyhose

From thick and snug to sleek and sexy, stockings have come a long way since their early ancestors, hose, which were in fashion in Europe in the 1500s. As early as 1566, Queen Elizabeth I of England received "a pair of black knit silk stockings for a new year's gift" from her silkwoman Mistress Montagu, after which she declared "henceforth I will weare no more cloth stockings," referring to a separate covering from the knee down.

The enduring popularity of silk stockings was challenged only by the introduction of new materials such as nylon and other man-made fibers in the 1940s, which provided the first durable, comfortable alternative to the luxury of silk. No hosier at the start of the twentieth century could have possibly imagined the choice of texture and pattern found on stockings and pantyhose as the 1990s drew to a close.

All the news that's fit to wear: both sexes celebrate (*above*) the debut of the stocking, a fashion accessory which, little did they know, would be around for many years to come. As sexy as it seams: Yves Saint Laurent turns nice girls naughty and naughty girls chic with his seriously seamed silhouettes (*right*).

The fabulous flapper: Sally O'Neill flaunts lace, patterned stockings (*above*) in the film *Sally, Irene and Mary*.

Beauty in a bottle: the new liquid stockings (*below*) quenched women's thirst for style during trying war times.

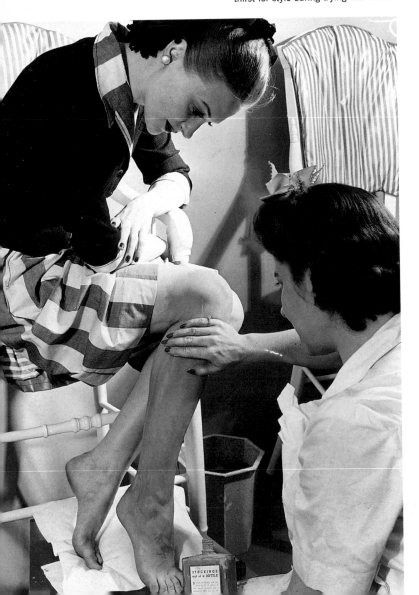

A ray of glamor: Hosiery gets done up in rayon like this brown and tan pair of stockings (*right*) from St. Margaret.

A LONG HISTORY

Short silk chemises and silk drawers worn over stockings that stretched to the knees, or corsets with suspenders (known as the basque) were all the rage in the early 1900s, although the poor had to resort to stockings tied below the knee with cord, tape, or bits of string. In 1913, in an age before rayon and other man-made fibers, schoolgirls on both sides of the Atlantic darned their stockings when they ran; the neatly mended pair would have lasted far longer than any schoolgirl's tights today. Even though the new silk and rayon stockings, developed with the use of modern technology, were to revolutionize the production of hosiery, they could not be salvaged as easily as earlier wool and silk pairs. When they ran or laddered they were often stitched into shoulder pads or other fashion accessories.

The role of the garter

The earlier stockings of this century were held up either with suspenders, attached to a corset or suspended from a belt at the waist, or with garters which gripped the leg. But in the 1920s, manufacturers dreamed up garters with ribbon rosettes which were worn beneath new short skirts; by 1928, suspender belts were a thing of the past as stockings were rolled around garters above the knee.

Unlike other forms of lingerie which was available according to each new trend that surfaced, stockings were seasonal wear. Black stockings were worn for winter and white for summer, although special pairs colored to go with a specific dress for evening were also popular. Many pairs were designed to expose legs, and women of the 1920s sought out versions in flesh colors, pink, beige, and fawn in the recently introduced rayon, or "art" (artificial) silk.

The new art silk stockings could be found on display at the 1925 Paris *Exposition des Art Decoratifs*, the launch pad for the influential decorative arts movement, Art Deco. Designers showed gold and silver stockings with feathers embroidered in colored silks and embellished with diamond bracelets or hand-sewn pearls at the ankle. In 1926, artists showed stockings that offered a veiled effect, especially in the form of women emerging from a car and baring their legs above their stockings. The flesh-colored nylons grew closer to nude, making the nylons look more and more transparent. They were worn rolled around the garter like a bracelet and highlighted the parts of the body that were bare to the waist. Because of this coy look, stockings took on an erotic overtone until the early 1930s, when suspender belts came back into vogue and the garter disappeared.

Changing hosiery for a changing world

The influence of Hollywood soon made itself felt in the stocking industry. In the 1930 film *The Blue Angel*, Marlene Dietrich wore them to play a temptress attempting to manipulate men's fantasies. Stockings also appeared in the novel *The Edwardians*, written by Englishwoman Vita Sackville-West, where they were worn as a version of power dressing: Viola watched her mother being dressed by her maid, who carefully drew on her silk stockings over her chemise and clipped her suspenders to them.

The younger generation continued to leave stockings to their elders, however, especially after the first nylons went on sale at stores throughout the United States on May 15, 1940. Some 4 million pairs were sold in just four days. But American women were forced to give up these newfound treasures once their country joined World War II—women in Europe, where the war had started earlier, were yet to experience the joys of "nylons"—despite their enthusiasm for the new fiber. During World War II, nylon production was commandeered for the war effort, and women reverted to using makeup to decorate their legs, drawing "seams" up the back with eyebrow pencil. When the war ended in 1945, nylons made their way back into stores but not fast enough. At Macy's, New York, the entire stock of 50,000 pairs sold out in six hours. In Pittsburgh, 40,000 women stood outside all night in the rain waiting to buy nylons from a tiny hosiery shop. By 1948, production had returned to normal and women could buy their stockings on a full night's sleep and in dry clothes.

Although fully-fashioned stockings were still available in silk, nylon quickly cornered the market. Stockings became known for their different weights, and women wore 30 denier for everyday wear and 15 denier for special occasions. The stiletto of 1951 drew attention to the shape of the ankle and calf and the move of a woman's hips as she walked. Skirts got shorter each year after the war, and thick lisle stockings that made legs look huge were discarded in exchange for white or colored silk versions or the still new flesh-colored options that imitated nudity. Instead of the old garter and stockings which were worn to above the knee with traditional garter belts, the latest stockings reached mid thigh and were created with a special band that prevented them from slipping down.

Nylon mixes arrive

In the late 1950s, nylon stockings were finer, and far cheaper, than ever before, as well as offering a much better shape than those made of other fabrics. The closer fit encouraged designers to raise dress hems in 1958 to an inch (2.5 cm) or so above the knee, and the bare-legged look of seamless nylons was introduced. By 1959, improved analine dying techniques meant that stockings in such bright colors as magenta were available to spruce up previously dull outfits while simultaneously lifting the spirits of those who wore them. The 1959 birth of Spandex, a fabric that continuously conforms to the body by stretching and snapping in place, made saggy baggy hose a distant memory.

Pantyhose became all the rage in the 1960s. These first "tights" were stockings that merged with panties knitted in thin natural rubber

Enmeshed in mesh: stockings take on a decorative edge as they've been woven in intricate patterns. Here, the mesh leg (*right*) looks smooth and sexy.

The human touch: Before modern technology, workers at local stocking factories (*left*) produced man-manufactured hosiery.

The sexy edge: Sheer nylons (*right*) showed off the skin and made the guys surrender. Women would slip them on and men would fall at their feet.

Unfair!

Better give yourself an unfair advantage with CHARNOS nylons

Something to snuggle up in: Women turned up the heat, even on the coldest winter days, with their thinck, woolen stockings (*above*).

threads. Legs were in vogue, especially when covered with sexy diamond-studded black seamed stockings or pantyhose in every color and texture. In 1969, Round-the-Clock introduced a silky Deering Miliken fabric which reinforced both thighs and tummy with its unique fibers knitted into the leg and abdominal area, and by winter of the same year, pantyhose were cut in Lycra tricot with net panties.

But stockings had not gone forever. Black seamed stockings and thin lacy garter belts came back with a vengeance in the 1970s, sold to define the figure with a definite erotic overtone. Disco attire and slit skirts revealed legs in a whole new way, and sexy hosiery was there to show them off. By 1977, designers were experimenting with any number of legwear styles, from fine white anklets and ribbed solid knee highs to the more mainstream dark or opaque tights which were easily rolled, cuffed, or slouched on the leg. Sonia Rykiel's pale tights caught the eye, as did Geoffrey Beene's rolled sock, Gianni Versace's cuffed sock, Oscar de la Renta's ribbed knee high, and Richard Assatly's pale leg tights. Bobby socks and striped anklets turned up from Hot Sox and Burlington, as legwear showed off its sexy side in sheer shades.

The appeal of texture

The late 1970s also brought about extensive design tactics and fabric mixes for pantyhose. Textures for warmer winter tights, including heavy diamond patterns in 100% nylon in a variety of colors could be seen. Two-tone seamless pinstripe tights in black and gray, camel and brown, tan and natural, and wine and slate were available from Danskin, while Burlington showed chain-linked weaves made of 100% nylon in terracotta, burgundy, taupe, green, and winter white. Berkshire's diamond pantyhose in black, navy, burgundy, cream, and taupe in 100% textured nylon turned up on legs everywhere.

Leg warmers enjoyed a vogue, made popular by the film *Flashdance* and were worn under skirts like leggings. Danskin, Burlington/Adler, and Trimfit all marketed leg warmers knitted in 100% wool.

But the most luxurious of all fabrics, silk, still had an edge over its rivals, as women of all ages continued to associate silk with classic elegance. Americans clamored for Dior's extra sheer two-thread silk stockings in champagne; imported from France. "I know of no facilities in America today for manufacturing silk stockings; it was an art that went out of the window about twenty years ago," claimed Louise Steconni, fashion director for Vision Hosiery and CD legwear. Steconni believed the generation which grew up surrounded by synthetic fabrics, had lost sight of silk, even though its naturalness made it an obvious choice for those who could not wear man-made fibers.

The seamier side of life

Seams continued to be as fashionable as in previous eras. The French hosiery firm Le Bourget made seamed pantyhose in black, taupe, and dark gray, creating a new kind of femininity for women. Jerry Horowitz, vice president of sales at Berkshire Hosiery, told *Women's Wear Daily* that the 1970s rage for seamed pantyhose started in the African-American community some six months before other women picked up on the trend.

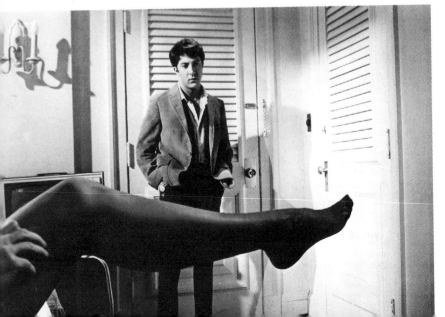

Stockings get sexy: Dustin Hoffman watches Mrs. Robinson slip into a pair of stockings (*left*) in the film *The Graduate*.

Toe jam: These striped knitted knee-highs (*right*) turn up with individually knitted toes so you can wiggle your way with style.

A strip of stripes: With a nod to the 70s and 80s, woolen tights (*left*) draw the line with seriously strong, colored stripes.

Garter belts came back in, and pin-up girls clad in sensually-inspired legwear posed sexily (or so they thought) for men's magazines. In one 1979 feature in *New York Magazine*, vintage World War II stockings were on display, albeit with extra sparkle and accentuated seams. Seamed hosiery was adopted by followers of the emerging disco scene. Berkshire's jet black, brown, and taupe pairs hit big in time for the Christmas season, along with Yves St Laurent's high-chic seamed look and any other dark, seamed pantyhose. Hot dot patterns in ultrasheer pantyhose, Le Bourget's reverse dots, and net pantyhose with dots were all labeled sexy items on the disco circuit, their design influenced by retro fashion.

In 1979, fishnets shown on Paris ready-to-wear catwalks rivaled the previous year's success for seams, as designers showed fishnets in black and rainbow colors. Berkshire's fishnets came in floral patterned black, berry, and cream nets.

It was becoming clear that earlier rules for legwear counted for naught as designers decided that anything went. Karen Davis' reptile looks featured tights in a knit of black scales made from Antron nylon and Lycra Spandex, with background colors of green, red, and purple (these doubled as skinny pants under a skirt for evening) while another 1970s trend, roller-skating, meant a huge calling for the required roller socks, or Pop Sox. Foxy Sox were brightly striped, knee-high acrylic versions sequined with pompoms, and Hot Sox, cotton and nylon terry knee-highs, turned up in yellow, apple, green, royal blue, and red, trimmed with white at the top and toe.

Colored silk stockings, knee highs, and anklets were created by the small American firm based in New York's SoHo now known as the Hue Accessory Company. Founded in the late 1970s, this company originally produced cotton stockings but soon switched to silk for luxury, warmth, and fit. At first they used transparent silk before changing to spun silk for an opaque look that was designed to go with elegant, sporty clothes. Hue's silk legs in cherry, natural black, turquoise, and gray were still popular in the 1990s.

Stockings for the Lycra age

Stockings were the ultimate fashion solution in the 1980s. Body stockings and pantyhose made from variable knits could smooth out body imperfections in hips, thighs, and calves, as the control top became part of the package. Designers began to use pantyhose to draw attention with designs in strategic places—Margaret Phillips created geometric patterns in purple and green up a white opaque leg, and Big Sky Montana used heat to transfer tattoos such as hearts with arrows onto sheer derrières, ankles, calves, or thighs. Danskin's Bonnie August created a circle chain rhinestone heart on the left leg of one seriously sheer pair of tights.

Shorter skirts and Bermuda shorts worn without boots put the spotlight on legs, especially in winter. Tights were knitted to look like fine tweed or herringbone and were worn with blanket coats, flannel skirts or angora sweaters. Ribbed

The bohemian look: Doc Marten boots worn with wooly tights (*left*) were trendsetters' late seventies/early eighties uniform of choice.

Fogal

For nearly 30 years, the high-quality hosiery produced by the Swiss company Fogal has been sought out by the world's most elegant women. As the wheels of fashion turned, Fogal and its hosiery went in and out of style, but as attention once again focused on the leg in the 1990s, Fogal enjoyed a cult status as a design label which represents both luxury and style.

Since the miniskirt of the 1960s drew the world's attention to legs in an unprecedented fashion, Fogal has made its name through its amazing range of colors—its hosiery has been produced in 115 standard colors, which never changed but were enhanced according to the color in vogue at the time. Each season its forecasters and designers offered new decorative themes to the public, including lacy weaves and patterns.

Fogal built its reputation on the quality of its products, which included pantyhose, stockings, garter belts, gartertop stockings, ladies' socks, and knee-highs, as well as matching lingerie, body stockings, and activewear. All have been marketed with great success, and Fogal also offers socks for men. As part of Fogal's determination to maintain its level of choice and service, it offers a selection of special sizes for wider hips or longer legs in addition to the standard sizes.

In total there are more than 120 different articles in Fogal's repertoire, more than two thirds of which are manufactured in Switzerland. As a country renowned for its textile industry and its dedication to outstanding quality, the company's Swiss label has proved an asset in most of the capitals of the world, where Fogal has highly visible stores in the fashionable shopping streets. Fogal's 64 shop windows can be relied on to show identical displays of merchandise at any one time, all of which are characterized by stylized legs and a rainbow of colors.

101

And then there were three . . .

In the spring of 1978, Take Three Inc. of Honolulu, under the name Tria and Take Three, introduced crotchless individual pantyhose. The idea was to slip on each leg separately since there was no connecting panty, and carry a third leg in a convenient plastic purse to use as a substitute in case one of the original legs acquired a run. The set ($3.95 for the trio) was composed on 15% and 18% tria denier nylon. The concept originated in Europe but was redeveloped in the United States in an attempt to get more use out of a pair of pantyhose, and to up its hygienic status. There was a medical benefit to the pantie-less version as well as a convenience factor: women never had to remove them for the ladies' room, a process which caused sagging when performed repetitively.

tights, colorful pantyhose, and patterned or textured leg warmers were also trendy, while those who preferred the preppie look called for crew socks. For winter lovers, there were shaggy rugged rag knit leg warmers from Izod in brushed wool and nylon blends of oatmeal, blueberry, and raspberry, and Foxy Sox leggings in a Peruvian look composed of crocheted acrylic and chenille in neutral tones. Changes in lifestyle demanded casual hosiery and body wear suitable for active women. A variety of colors and styles coordinated with the rapid fashion changes of the early 1980s, and regular stockings gave way to pantyhose as the popularity of pants and slacks increased. But both were replaced to some extent by sheer knee-highs and other types of socks.

Women shopped for their hosiery at supermarkets and retail outlets where they could find lower-priced pantyhose, and shop more conveniently than in traditional stores. The department stores still offered a larger variety of legwear and the latest designs, including new products such as control top and sheer support hose were often worn as the first layer of the favored many-layered look of the day. But nonetheless, one in four women bought at discount prices. Manufacturers felt that frequent line changes were necessary to ensure a competitive edge in department stores and specialty outlets, and designer and private labels encouraged many women to develop a loyalty to specific hosiery brands. Tights grew ever more daring, appearing with wildcat prints, cheetah black spots on sheer orange backgrounds, black tiger stripes, and silver and bronze cotton anklets. Metallic threads, trellis lace patterns, and gold and silver edges came into play for evening wear, while others were trimmed in delicate floral lace with shimmering metallic touches. Among the most luxurious of these novelty lines were Fogal's black seamed sheer nylon hosiery with delicate bow patterns, Electric Sok's cotton and nylon thigh-highs with lavender metallic threads, and Dim's black nylon legwear with dots and a lace band at the top.

The return of glamor

As the 1980s progressed, textured ultrafeminine nylons became all the rage. Sheer black with floral patterns and textures, flocked ankle treatments, and Lycra Spandex ultrasheer pantyhose and knee-highs were often sold with traditional items such as bras or lacy briefs. Just as the revival of the miniskirt called for pantyhose and tights, the reintroduction of longer skirts demanded thigh-highs and over-the-knee looks; all in fashionable sheer hosiery. The growth of athletic footwear, as well as the market for streetwear and fitness trends, pushed the sock trade into the limelight. Lycra Spandex cotton took over the industry, and many leg coverings were decorated with boldly painted or subtly patterned designs. But stockings and tights remained, as they had always been, a staple of women's wardrobes. By 1990, women could buy stockings and tights in any color or weight (the per capita women's hosiery consumption rose from 20 to 24 pairs that year,) with a new interest by younger women in stockings. Previously thought of as for the older generation, stockings again became glamor items, worn with sexy garter belts—or on their own, thanks to integral garters which held them up. Eclectic hosiery designs were seen in the Paris collections of the early 1990s, when models wore two or three pairs of pantyhose to create a subtly colored effect. Christian Lacroix showed handpainted tights in abstract patterns, and Emilio Pucci produced intricate multicolored patterns and explosive decorative prints leading to a revival of Op Art stripes and checks. Many imitation abstract patterns followed from young designers, and manufacturers began using recycled natural fibers in neutral colors, such as 100% recycled cotton, raw silk or linen dyed with vegetable pigments. In the late 1990s, natural legwear in rich textures were the lines women turned to. Manmade fibers had revolutionized the hosiery trade, which began the century with ill-fitting silk or wool stockings and finished with lightweight, sag-free stockings and tights.

Big screen glamor: inspired by hot Hollywood stars, stockings, suspenders and fluffy, high-heeled mules (*below*) made fashion history.

Stockings—a brief history

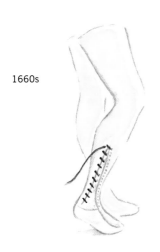

1660s

Stockings are not a recent invention. By the earliest centuries A.D., most Europeans covered their legs with rough-fitting knitted or woven trousers which stretched to the ankle. These were known as *hose*, meaning a covering for the legs in Old German. Chausses were also popular, rudimentary stockings which were crisscrossed with gartering for decoration, some of which covered the foot, others stopping at the ankle.

From around 1340, hose came to refer to two long stockings, mainly worn by men, which were cut to fit the leg tightly from crotch to foot. These were sometimes lined with fur for extra warmth and had soled feet, worn indoors in place of shoes.

By the early 1500s, hose were often divided into two parts. The bottom half were fitted and gartered at the knee, and became known as stocks, or netherstocks. A century later, netherstocks were widely worn by men with trunk hose, fashionable short, full knickerbockers that originated in Spain. These knickerbockers later developed into looser breeches which were worn with stockings held in place just below the knee with garters.

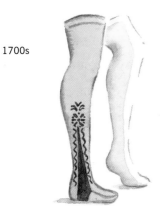

1700s

By the 1600s, England held the monopoly on European hose production, thanks to the invention in 1589 of a manual stocking knitting frame by one William Lee. More than six times faster than a skilled hand knitter, this machine could produce 600 stitches per minute using the same principles employed by today's high-performance knitting machines.

By 1860, hosiery production was mechanized. The knitting frame of the late 1800s was quickly followed by the cotton machine, which manufactured flat knit stockings in the shape of the leg, closed by a seam; up to 40 seamed stockings could be produced at the same time.

As skirt hems rose in the early 1900s, soft, transparent, and durable stockings came into vogue, much aided by the development of the first rayons, or "artificial silk." A range of manmade fibers followed, leading to Dupont's first nylon stockings in 1938 and Bayer's Perlon stockings.

Shortly after World War II the arrival of the circular knitting machine brought seamless stockings and the demise of the cotton machine, and before long, pantyhose or tights had overtaken stockings as the leg covering of choice, especially when worn with the 1960s mini skirt. Fashion demanded different colors and patterns, too.

In the 1980s Lycra revolutionized the fit of tights and stockings, making the yarns hug and shape the legs. Its phenomenal properties meant Lycra appeared in all forms of hosiery thereafter, from tights and conventional stockings with suspenders, to hold-ups and pop socks.

1860s

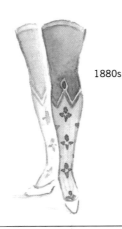

1880s

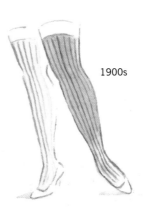

1900s

1920s

103

Mary Quant

From the moment she opened her boutique Bazaar on London's King's Road in 1955, Mary Quant's fashions, underwear, and cosmetics became the icons of a generation. Her styling of the miniskirt spearheaded a fashion revolution in the Swinging Sixties, creating a new look reminiscent of the flat-chested, boyish ideal of the 1920s, but with a lively dynamism of its own.

Music from the master: Mary Quant's magic made lingerie history. From boy-spirited bras and panties to Twiggy-inspired bodysuits and brilliantly basic accessories (*above*), her English edged looks drew a dedicated following at home and overseas.

The simple daisy motif Mary Quant used since her first ground-breaking fashion designs hit the streets of London in the 1950s had become an instantly recognized international icon for her brands by the late 1990s.

Quant's youthful style was quickly adopted by dedicated followers of fashion, photographers, hairdressers, and models alike. Hairdresser Vidal Sassoon created the distinctive, angular haircut worn by all and sundry, while tall, willowy fashion models such as Twiggy sported the sleeveless, crochet tops and skinny rib sweaters that turned their backs on the padded, pointy breasts of the 1950s.

But although Mary Quant is often credited with inventing the miniskirt and tights, this is not the case. French designer André Courrèges first lifted hemlines above the knee, and the designer Balençiaga first introduced brightly-colored tights. In both cases, however, Quant's interpretations of these moves were more daring than the original. And as Quant's miniskirt and hot pants made stockings and garters obsolete, tights became essential wear for most of the female population.

When Quant introduced tights into her collection in 1965, it set another fashion landmark, although today, when tights are an essential part of many women's wardrobe, it is hard to imagine. Quant was equally at home designing such necessary underwear as she was outerwear, explaining to American *Vogue* in 1995 that "I have always thought that it is important to have a look from top to toe—it's all the pieces that make up the whole. For me it was the tights that were so important to complete the look with very simple dresses, the elongated cardigans, knickerbockers, and bloomers. Everyone wanted those tights. People didn't make tights then except for the theater so I did have a job persuading the manufacturers to make them. We've had licences ever since then because it worked so well."

With her business partners, Archie McNair and Alexander Plunkett Green (whom she married in 1957), Quant went on to build a fashion empire. Although they soon opened another branch of Bazaar in London—the store was designed by young interior designer Terence Conran—they recognized that Bazaar's relatively expensive clothes would not sustain the business. So in 1961 Quant went wholesale. "It is pointless in fashion to create a couture design and imagine it can be adequately produced in quantity," said Quant. "Fashion must be created from the start for mass production with full knowledge of mass-production methods."

In 1962, a major American retailer, J. C. Penney, signed Mary Quant to design underwear for their 1,700 American stores, the first of many such contracts.

By 1965, she was also designing for Lecore in the Netherlands, and Arnbergs Fabriksaktiebolag in Sweden, for example. But she had not abandoned her own business. In 1963 Quant's "Ginger Group" was launched, which introduced a new concept of coordinated separates, dresses, and sportswear for worldwide, international distribution. Rainwear and tights were introduced in 1965—that were later extended into branded stockings and underwear—and within seven years of opening the first boutique, Mary Quant's clothes were available in Britain, the U.S., France, Italy, Switzerland, Kenya, South Africa, Australia, and Canada.

By the end of the 1990s, the Quant empire enjoyed a turnover in excess of £150 million, with Japan being the group's largest market. There, more than two hundred "Mary Quant Colour" boutiques combined fashion, fashion accessories, and cosmetics. As the designer most responsible for mass merchandising of modern fashion, and the emergence of the international designer label, Quant has become an archetype for contemporary style, and design. Her originality shines through in her brave, original designs and attention-grabbing pronouncements, including her remark that "I love vulgarity. Good taste is death, vulgarity is life."

In print: Quant illustrates her good taste in printed bras and matching panties (*above*)— lazy enough to lounge in at home but confident enough to go out under the latest fashions.

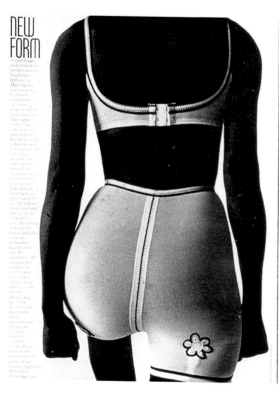

NEW FORM

In full bloom: Quant's signature daisy turned up when you least expected it to—the funky flower (*left*) makes its mark on the back of her sportswear-inspired briefs shown here with bra tops.

Berlei

Berlei, one of the fastest growing lingerie brands in the world, has more than sixty years of experience in the design and manufacture of quality women's underwear. From its humble beginnings in the back streets of Sydney, Australia, Berlei has grown without ever losing its initial philosophy—"to design, manufacture and sell corsets and brassières of such perfect fit, quality and workmanship as will bring pleasure and profit to all concerned."

The origins of the Berlei company lie in a romance between the owner of a small corsetry company, Mabel Mobberley, and her then accountant, Fred Burley. Their subsequent marriage led to the foundation of the Berlei company in 1917.

By 1923, Berlei had expanded their business as far as Europe, opening prestigious offices in the Liberty building in London's stylish Regent Street. Once there, the company specialized in top-of-the-range exclusive designs. Following the outbreak of World War II in 1939, Berlei's manufacturing plant made a range of Utility brassières and girdles for the forces. It was one of the few companies allowed to put its brand name in the garments, creating a loyal following that maintained for at least a decade.

A highly innovative company, Berlei has always had a tradition of thoroughly understanding its consumers; after an intensive research project in 1926, carried out nationwide in Australia, for example, it was the first company, in collaboration with Sydney University, to identify and classify the five standard figure types for women. Nonetheless, Berlei's fortunes declined through the 1950s and 1960s, until the company nearly disappeared when it went into receivership in the mid 1970s.

Berlei was subsequently owned by a succession of companies until it was purchased by Courtaulds Textiles in 1986, a move which led to the hugely successful "Shock Absorber" and "Answers" collections. Such market success clearly demonstrates how in tune Berlei is with key consumer needs, its recognition that women come in all shapes and sizes reflected in the breadth of its size ranges.

Ready for work: Berlei's utility bra and girdle (*above*), designed in 1941 for the women's forces, was made with elastic materials that eliminated the use of pre-war boned fabrics.

Straps get the shift: Berlei's designs (*left*) save women from embarassing strap display. Whether backless or strapless, their secret's safe with this brand.

Elbeo and Pretty Polly

By 1990, until it was purchased by the American Sara Lee Corporation, the Bahner family had been manufacturing stockings for some 250 years. Their company, Elbeo, was the oldest branded hosiery company in the world, and renowned for its support hose. In 1993, Elbeo merged with Pretty Polly, makers of fashion hosiery that was also owned by Sara Lee.

A smooth solution: Thanks to firming tummy panel, Pretty Polly's secret slimmer (*right*) streamlines the body into a curvaceous, sexy silhouette.

Originally founded in 1741 in Oberlungwitz in Germany by Johann Christian Bahner, it was Louis Bahner, who took over the business in 1906. Determined to provide a guarantee of quality to his customers, he began marking his initials (L.B.O., or Louis Bahner Oberlungwitz) on his products, and it was from this that the Elbeo brand name was born.

The superior quality of Elbeo's stockings quickly gained international recognition at the 1937 World Exhibition in Paris. Indeed, Elbeo was awarded the *Grand Prix*, the only hosiery company ever to receive this honor.

It is Elbeo's expertise in support hosiery, developed over forty years, which made the company's name. Its unrivaled standard for support hose was perfected after Elbeo developed a working relationship with The Queen's Medical Centre in Nottingham, England. In 1958 Elbeo established a subsidiary company in Britain, manufacturing from a factory in Cumbria, to meet British demand. So successful was the venture that in 1965 it opened a head office in Nottingham, the British town most famous for hosiery and lace. Further expansion included a new factory in Cumbria and the acquisition of the Martyn Fisher factory in Sutton in Ashfield, Nottinghamshire, England, where Jacquard knitting machines made the unique patterns for Elbeo's products.

During the 1990s, Elbeo's fashion hosiery took off. The Shimmering Sheer collection was launched in 1992, and just a year later, the sub-brand Seasons offered high quality opaques and textured hosiery in top fashion colors. Sheer Extravagance, of 1994, was launched for the luxury market.

Pretty Polly pulls

The Pretty Polly brand was originally named after a famous racehorse, owned by a English bookmaker. His daughter established a hosiery wholesaling company in Sutton in Ashfield, and in 1926 the business was taken over by Hibbert and Buckland, a local hosiery manufacturer. Its new owners developed the brand, together with its famous parrot trademark, and by the 1930s Pretty Polly was famous for high-quality stockings made from silk, nylon, and lisle. In 1939, its annual sales of fine-gauge hosiery was over 48 million pairs.

In 1959, company ownership changed again. Now part of the Thomas Tilling Group, its name was officially listed as Pretty Polly Ltd, and within a year Pretty Polly introduced the first non-run seamfree stockings. This innovative move was echoed a decade later when Hold Ups were launched, eliminating the need for a garter belt. Soon afterward, one-size stockings were followed by one-piece tights—essential to wear with the mini-skirt. Sheer Knee Highs were the solution for 1970s tight jeans.

As hosiery made a revival during the 1980s, Pretty Polly introduced Lycra into its 15 denier range. It was the first to combine ultrafine Lycra with a fine-dernier, textured yarn. Its famous "Nylons" of 1988, still the company's bestseller, were equally trendsetting, heralding the vogue for a sheer look.

In 1991 the Sara Lee Corporation, already owning Elbeo, bought Pretty Polly—the year the company achieved a world first by using microfibers in sheer and opaque hosiery—and then merged the two companies in 1993, resulting in the control of over twenty-three percent of the world's hosiery market by the late 1990s. Since then, the company, operating under the Pretty Polly name, has received an accolade for being the first to produce the finest sheer 5 denier hosiery, while other products have been supported by innovative advertising.

Bedroom Lingerie

8

After centuries of sleeping in the nude, it was in the 1500s that women started wearing nightgowns. They still received visitors in bed well into the 1600s—the bedroom was a place for lounging so nightgowns and overlaying transparent robes were worn late in the

day. The less modest *casaquin*, which looked like a corset with petticoats attached from the waist down and left breasts and legs uncovered, was ousted in the 1800s by the starched, laced, or buttoned-up nightdresses which enveloped women from the neck to the wrists and ankles. But by the time the twentieth century rolled around, bedroom attire took a turn toward a whole new style of dressing, set for a radical change as social mores relaxed.

Under cover: Women's bed clothes (*above*) get buttoned up and draped down for a far from sexy effect.
Feeling naughty? Slip into Janet Reger's brown floral patterned negligée with an overlaying wrap.

BOUDOIR GLAMOR

In the first years of the 1900s, sleepwear, as with all forms of clothing, was ostentatiously ornate, and negligées, boudoir gowns, and tea gowns were laden down with decoration, with a total disregard for practicality. Anything luxurious became the desire of every wealthy woman. "Almost any young girl will confess," noted *Vogue* in 1916, "that her greatest weakness is for the pretty things of the boudoir. Nothing caresses her to the same purring delight as a soft silken *peignoir* or a fluffy *matinée*."

Gowns were worn within the intimate four walls of the home, and there were plenty of styles to choose from. Women opted for tea gowns in old gold satin which came with hoods of cream net lace and blue velvet bows, or informal dinner *negligées* caped in skunk-edged, jewel-embroidered net over layered *charmeuse*. The *saut de lit*, a silk slip to throw over the nightgown when a woman emerged from the bedroom, was another staple. Heavily embroidered tea gowns with trains in lacy pastels were worn over corsets for entertaining the most intimate friends. After white, pink was the color that washed best, and flannelette models in pink and blue stripes were popular. During wartime, however, nightgowns became less bulky, losing their elaborate frills, tucking, and embroidery. World War I produced a vogue for pajamas, too, which resembled men's models and were cut in a variety of sometimes-striped fabrics. Many pajamas were sold with night caps, sleeping nets, and lace boudoir caps, as well as Shetland wool sleeping socks. But although they were comfortable and good value, it took a while for pajamas to catch on since garments with any kind of masculine association were considered unfashionable. By the late 1920s, however, tailored pajamas were seen everywhere, with novelty pajamas encouraging new and innovative lingerie pieces.

Oriental influences prevailed in the early part of the decade, and by 1926, artificial silks (rayons) such as ultrafine crêpe, lockstitch, and other finer fabrics were being used on colorful nightwear. Printed chiffon and crêpe pajamas turned up bright and bold. Traveling had become one of America's favorite pastimes, and so popular that couture houses even made sleeping bags, coverlets, pillows, and sheets to match their lingerie sets. "The smart woman," said *Vogue*, "travels with lovely lingerie and amusing pajamas in her train."

Beyond beige: Complex details like a drawn waist and pink lace on the chest give this 1920s pajama set (*right*) added interest.

Royal nights: A pale green silk dressing gown (*left*) with a white and gold collar gets a touch of royalty as its sleeves are trimmed in an intricately stitched pattern.

Streamlined styles were a hit as women wore long nightgowns with embroidered yokes. Under light dresses or *negligées*, the popular attire was another matching set of a long-sleeved nightshirt, or chemise, and panties. Nightwear was also important for reading in bed; propped up on lacy pillows, women looked much more elegant and felt more comfortable wearing bright buttoned-up nightshirts.

Black lace made its debut during the 1920s, revealing sexily clad figures that were meant to be displayed. Gossamer's black chemise, for example, was cut from layers of fine chiffon, using black lace for the bodice and hem, and double-faced satin ribbon straps.

Such items were covered with any number of overjackets, including luxurious breakfast jackets, another addition to bedroom attire. These were made of fabrics such as the softest velvet, lined in chiffon and trimmed with fur. When worn with a Dutch cap of ecru net and lace and tied with silk ribbons, it became a definite fashion statement.

Postwar freedoms

With the growing femininity of the 1930s came the nightgown modeled after the bias-cut evening dress. Often made in transparent materials, this outlined the body, featuring a low neck and gaping side, and was worn with additional garments such as short coats or boleros, with sleeves similar to those of evening dresses. Nightgown skirts were lengthened and expanded with pleats, imitating the design of an evening dress, while masculine pajama trousers, previously with legs, swelled out from the knee down to simulate a skirt.

Lingerie gowns were narrower and more revealing in the 1930s, and featured low, rounded, or v-necks, made of transparent fabrics with silk linings and matching shawls threaded with silver. Scraps of fabric were stitched together to create bed jackets, edged with swans' down, lace bands, or silk velvet capes.

Toward the end of the 1930s, lighter fabrics such as silk and chiffon came into vogue for nightgowns, now nicknamed "nighties," which were often worn with boudoir caps. These finer fabrics were easy to launder during wartime, a time when nightgowns were cut radically shorter, and were often lighter, flowing, and more transparent.

"One of the most glamorous women I ever met had no makeup on her face, was wearing corduroy trousers and sewing a chiffon night-gown," claimed Judy Campbell ("Glamour Is What You Make It," *Vogue* 1941). Nightgowns imitated evening gowns in black georgette, fine silks, and satins, with full skirts that touched the ground or reached mid calf. The bodices were fitted, low backed or halter necked, elegant and formal, and served as a nightgown or when dressed up with a fashionable bolero or bed jacket, sophisticated attire for intimate dinners at home.

Evening entertainment...all day long: It was customary to wear your evening wear, such as this smoking jacket (*above*) no matter what time of day.

A winning battle: After the war, lingerie loosened up. This 1923 ensemble (*top left*) comes with a flowing negligée and draped wrap.

Star-inspired silhouettes: Sexy pieces showed up for bedtime as early as 1923, like this negligée outfit (*left*) with slip and wrap.

Dressed to kill: A 1938 peach silk nightie (*above*) decorated with a silk georgette front panel.

Wartime reality

But such escapism was hard to maintain as World War II dragged on. Times were rough and there was scarce need for luxurious lingerie. If glamor was ever on the agenda for evening, European women often found their bubbles burst by the prospect of a night spent in an air raid shelter, sitting up in a chair or being rudely awakened at any hour and rushing to slip into something serviceable.

In Britain, the most practical solutions came from the Army and Navy store catalog, which advertised a wool flannel Wincey suitable for day and night wear as well as nightdresses with low rounded necks, front fastening, scalloped edges, and embroidered white or colored cotton with sleeves. Dresses were a major influence, as one Bestway pattern for a nightdress that appeared in *Wife and Home* in 1942 showed. It closely resembled a yellow satin evening dress from 1932.

Also in 1942, manufacturers introduced a summer sleeping garment which had short trousers, and elastic insets at each side of the back adjusted the waist to the wearer. Even *Vogue* joined the practical bandwagon for a while, advertising a pattern for an all-in-one pajama step-in with a front fastening of buttons or zipper, and wide legs that could be gathered at the ankles for comfort. When hooded, this suit could serve as a shelter or siren suit.

Nightwear grew even more feminine, with layers and layers of nylon, lace that billowed down the front of the gown from neck to hem, and nylon frills around the edges. Even cotton got a little sexier, as layered hooded gowns made from embroidered cotton boasted wisps of silk *mousseline*, high waists, and very low ruffled necklines. Puffed and gathered sleeves, whether short or elbow length, were very popular for nightgowns and negligées, while housecoats in pastel stripes and flower prints with wide-yoked necklines imitated the fashionable *décolletage*.

Peacetime pleasures

At the end of World War II in 1945, the demure *negligée* with high neck and long sleeves was high fashion, and before long, the slimline slip with no ornamentation but a dash of nylon chiffon around the hem followed suit. American *Vogue* declared in 1946, "After the austere years of unpretty lingerie we can have it once again frilled and be-ribboned in the feminine way."

Stretch corsets were worn under nylon lace-trimmed *negligées* with fashionable frilly sleeves, finished with detail in gathered rayon and satin. Frills, lace *appliqués*, puffed sleeves, and gathered wrists added luxury to a cut that continued to accentuate the natural figure.

Elegant and frivolous pajamas were also in vogue, as women wore them out to buy groceries without a second thought. The once simple pieces had gained enormous chic and popularity, printed tops with matching plain green man-tailored slacks, perhaps with a female-friendly lamé collar and cuffs or with softly fluted, fine *mousseline* necklines. There were pajamas for beachwear, evening wear, and sportswear, as well as for lingerie.

From the end of World War II in 1945, women had taken to wearing pajama tops or jackets alone, and in response, designers began to create short nightgowns that reached the top of the thigh in light, transparent fabrics. For the first time in generations, sleeping in the nude, or as good as, was embraced again by many women.

Like most other forms of lingerie, nightwear ran the gamut in the 1950s, from the most covered-up pajamas and nightgowns to the sexiest little pieces. By mid decade, there were striped tunics in sheer nylon and white organza as well as pink satin peignoir sets from Ruth Flamm, which were ruffled at the neck and sashed below the bodice, and Dr. Zhivago-inspired form-fitting, feminine off-the-shoulder dresses.

Nancy Melcher's clinging translucent permanently pleated nylon nightgowns revolutionized the bedroom with designs that could be both sexy and sweet. West Coast lingerie was shocking and glamorous, Hollywood-style. Movie queens paraded around on big screens with slit-to-the-waist dressing gowns and leopard prints, the strategically placed openings highlighting sexual areas. Instead of resembling evening gowns, nightgowns were girlish, featuring high necks and petticoat-inspired details.

Some of the most innovative and dramatic lingerie pieces were pretty enough to party in, and as always, Hollywood was partly responsible. Virginia Wallace's delicate white tricot coat with billed sleeves and hem, French lace, and blue satin bows; Odette Barsa's white antique satin coat; and Rudolph Valentino's gold-struck embroidered Orlon in regal purple, pink, lavender, and green were considered stylish, and could have jumped off the silver screen. There were cobalt blues, silvery whites, and mulberry on flowing, softly draped robes from Tintoretto, and delicate Sylvia Pedlar breakfast coats turned up in multifloral eyelet cotton.

Glitz and glamor: This 1940s M&S nightie (*right*) gave women an especially dressy feel.

Hollywood's heyday: Lingerie makes it to the big screen. Betty Grable dons a silk dressing gown (*far right*) tied at the waist, and with a diamond triangular clasp at the cleavage.

Feeling frilly? Check out Gossard "Serenity" pink wrap robe (*left*) with pleated sheer nylon ruffles, pretty enough to wear to a party.

Recipe for glamor: A black negligée (*far left*) is the perfect uniform for this 1963 housewife who dresses up to cook dinner as her hair dries.

Be my baby: Girlish glamor in a grown-up size is illustrated here by this red baby doll nightie (*right*).

Who's Got The Action? Lana Turner certainly does in this $750 negligée (*below*) by Edith Head which she wore in the film by the same name. Made from embroidered Parisian Alencon lace, the gown is shaded by two layers of sheer *souffle de soie* and dyed the exact color of the star's skin.

Keeping it casual

Once women had realized they could find value, fashion, and quality at reasonable prices at department stores—by the onset of the 1960s—lingerie and nightwear quickly came out of the closet. Striking robes doubled as evening coats to be worn to the theater, the opera, or dinner parties, and sleepwear appeared at the beach, on the tennis court, or at the market. The sash became important, essential to create shape with garments that were mainly loose, rather than fitted and flared.

In response, a new line in nightwear appeared, and it became lighthearted and frilly. These sexy new pieces boasted all volume and no weight, as the most luxurious nightdresses and dressing gowns were made from the sheerest voile and chiffons. Full dressing gowns in colors such as peach, turquoise, azure, pink, or white, finished with frills and colored ribbons, created matching bedroom sets.

Women took to them, and they appeared in all colors and forms; pleating remained fashionable, and stripes and flower prints in pastel tones had invaded the bedroom by the middle of the decade. Nylon was appreciated for its lightness and drying speed, and because it was by now so enchantingly pretty. Other elasticized fabrics grew lighter and were used for complete foundation garments in soft colors such as coffee, tea, rose, turquoise, coral, pinks, and peach, incorporated into soft flower prints and candy stripes.

As the 1960s progressed, luxury nightwear became a melange of great fabrics and marvelous details, as did other clothes fashions. Bare skin was in and designs took on an extravagant edge. Exotic robes were padded and quilted with raised surfaces sporting polka dots, paisleys, and flowers in cotton and satin— Lanz of Salzburg in Los Angeles turned out a navy cotton quilted robe with a multicolored paisley print border and a long Victorian robe of acrylic and cotton in multicolored flowers—and short robes of quilted white satin, such as the model decorated with black polka dots from Odette Barsa, appeared.

Simply beautiful: This 1970s M&S nylon brown nightie (*above*) gives the wearer a dazzling edge with a brown embroidered top.

A modern approach

As cotton and nylon blends such as Dacron, which looked like freshly ironed cotton but needed little ironing, grew in popularity in the 1970s, pure nylon nightdresses faded away. Silk and wool mixes and crêpe were used for nightgowns, and chiffons and georgettes for matching *peignoirs*. Long, slim, square-necked nightgowns could still be found in women's lingerie drawers, but Baby Dolls, which *Vogue* described as "little cotton short suits that were lightly frilled and ruffled", became the latest in night dressing.

Baby Doll nightdresses that had first appeared in the 1960s boasted sexy necklines, like those of a camisole, or were gathered in dotted cotton, eyelet lace, Indian and jazzy prints with ribbons and bows. Considered high fashion, such nightgowns were usually worn without briefs, although coordinated underwear and nightwear in matching prints, *appliqués* or cutouts were also popular.

Plain colored cotton look-alikes, such as silk, wool, and chiffon, were later supplemented by psychedelic prints, introducing what *Vogue* called a "pulse-beat brilliance" to nightwear as the 1980s drew on. The frilly Baby Dolls were replaced by long soft jersey or chiffon nightdresses although women had begun to adopt a more unisex look as early as the mid 1970s. "Think of yourself in a rough soft warm pair of men's pajamas," advised British *Vogue* in 1974.

Luxurious pajamas had appeared in silk, cotton, wool, and cotton mixes in the early 1970s, and then in fine cotton jersey and silk jersey later in the decade. As the tranquil colors used at the start of the century made a comeback—white, flesh, coffee, black, and pinky mauves—contrasting colored embroidery was used to create striking designs. Toward the end of the 1980s, however, such subtle shades were replaced with the stronger burnt orange, turquoise, fuchsia, peach, apricot, pastel blues, and olive green.

Think pink: A black basque with suspenders (*far right*) gets a dose of color when paired with a pink negligée and fluffy pink slippers.

Seeing things clearly: At Knickerbox, a designer shop in the UK, women could find this black see-through, full-length nightie (*right*) that revealed their innermost features.

The extravagance of luxurious lingerie led to high prices, but in a period when excessive spending was the mood of the day, consumers bought them regardless. When the inevitable occured, and a period of recession hit most wealthy Western economies during the 1980s, retailers were forced to rethink their manufacturing policies. Fortunately, however, the prosperous 1990s were just around the corner.

The final say

The 1990s brought with them a more sophisticated sense of function and value. This new enthusiasm was the perfect complement to the increasingly popular at-home lifestyle, brought about by corporate cutbacks which forced women to build their own businesses and work at home while raising their kids. "Women think of the home as their castle," says David Komar, executive vice president of Komar Sleepwear. "They care what they wear at home."

Sheer luxury: Whether dressing for themselves or for their significant other, women adored sexy pieces like this Flora Nikrooz see-through floral patterned nightie (*right*) and delicate wrap.

What they were wearing were new fabrics such as polar fleece and other synthetics, but above all, cotton. Cotton knits appeared as sleepwear, underwear, and overwear, in T-shirts, leggings, vests, and jumpsuits. The sleepwear market expanded to include what people put on when they went home, which was not necessarily what they slept in.

According to Monica Mitro, director of public relations for the lingerie firm Victoria's Secret in the late 1990s, "Lingerie and sleepwear…transcended into a part of a woman's wardrobe," becoming more than just foundations. Women may have had a drawer full of nightclothes but they still wanted to own the newest models, colors, or style on the market. In addition, women wanted to look sexy but without being uncomfortable. In the late 1990s, they could have both; fine-quality gowns with matching robes that were beautiful to sleep in, but which they could also answer the door in.

Comfort, simplicity, and at times a decidedly feminine edge dominated sleepwear designs from companies such as Shadow Boxer and Joe Boxer. The J. Crew catalog advertised rugged flannels and basic cotton boxers, halterneck nightgowns, and cozy robes, while the famous Victoria's Secret book featured the sexiest silk, flannel, and corduroy lingerie on the market, as well as satin and cotton nightgowns, thermal cropped top and boxer short sets, and georgette and mesh gowns for the ideal romantic evening.

Such companies were pointing the way for sleepwear of the next century, the designs of which are likely to be equally functional yet sexy. As lingerie fabrics become increasingly soft, developed along the lines of the ultrasoft micro fibers and triple brushed flannels of the 1990s, sleepwear is likely to get cheaper, too. Definitely something to look forward to in the next millennium.

Victoria's Secret

The success of Victoria's Secret, an American company run by women for women, is a testament to mail order catalog selling. Since its formation in the early 1970s, the company's name has become synonymous with glamorous, romantic, indulgent and feminine lingerie, selling over six hundred items of underwear in every minute of every day.

One key reason for the success of Victoria's Secret is the fact that the company spreads its net so wide. Its president, Grace Nichols, describes the company as "a lifestyle business—and a fashion business, an integral part of our customers' lives. We offer our customers glamor, beauty, fashion, and a little bit of romance. We know what fits women physically and emotionally."

The company's Catalog division promotes a remarkably extensive range of lingerie and related clothing, with different specialty books for each of the different clothing styles. The Country, City, and Swim editions all cover lingerie to wear with the appropriate outer clothes, while the Christmas Dreams & Fantasies Catalog covers underwear for a special occasion. Literally millions of women recognize the name Victoria's Secret, with over 360 million copies of their catalogs circulated annually. The company is continually searching for new markets, expanding into Japan for example; by the end of the 1990s, Japanese women accounted for some 15% of total catalog sales.

The company is very much of its time, and is, quite literally, a women's business. Since its inception in the early 1970s, Victoria's Secret has seen remarkable growth, with annual sales exceeding $3 billion by the late 1990s. This phenomenal growth rate has been presided over by a workforce made up of eighty percent women, from its president and executive committee through to its sales representatives.

But although the company owes much of its success to its mail order side, there is also a huge range of stores owned by the company both in America and further afield. By 1997, Victoria's Secret stores in the United States offered a continually expanding range of luxurious bras, panties, sleepwear, and accessories, with

Diamonds are a girl's best friend: Model Claudia Schiffer exposes her extravagant side in the Million Dollar Miracle Bra and black gown (*right*).

bras and panties alone representing some twenty percent of the company's sales.

Victoria's Secret's design team has established a highly successful track record, introducing such new product lines as Second Skin Satin, Underware (cotton basics) Sensual Shapers, and the Perfect Silhouette. The company's bras in particular have sold so well that Victoria's Secret plans to launch a new bra style every year: it is estimated that women under the age of thirty buy some fifty percent of their bras from Victoria's Secret. Among its most memorable designs was the Million Dollar Miracle Bra, which was modeled by Claudia Shiffer on the cover of their Christmas Dreams & Fantasies Catalog.

Victoria's Secret's Annual Spring Fashion Show is held every February in New York, bringing to life the supermodels such as Tyra Banks who have been seen in the chain's catalogs by some 500 million customers around the world. This catwalk show also acts as an effective marketing tool for Victoria's Secret's own brand stores, including those which sell its signatory hosiery lines. By 1997, there were some fourteen hosiery stores, 750 Victoria's Secret stores and 119 dedicated Cacique stores in the United States alone, with more planned.

Cacique, the latest addition to Intimate Brands Inc, which owns

Victoria's Secret, has its own design team based in New York—this offshoot of the company was especially created to offer a new range of French-inspired designs for elegant and sophisticated lingerie. Targeted at the "intelligent woman," Cacique was the first in the world to market its T-shirt bra, which quickly established the new line as a global force to be reckoned with.

Intimate Brands Inc is listed on the New York Stock Exchange, and is a conglomerate of companies that includes Bath & Body Works (a specialty retailer for personal care products) and Gryphon, which designs, develops, formulates and sources toiletries, as well

as Victoria's Secret. There is a natural synergy between these related companies which contributes to the extremely successful performance of the group as a whole. The shrewd marketing campaign behind Intimate Brands Inc has made the most of Victoria's Secret's beautiful, romantic, lingerie, their impressive sales record confirming that women are still looking for intimate garments that promote a feeling of sensuality and well-being.

Miracle of miracles: Uplifting women's spirits as much as their bustlines, the Miracle Bra (*right*) added glamor to women's daily lives.

Janet Reger

The story of Janet Reger, the British designer, reads like a fairytale. It covers her rise to international fame as "the Queen of Luxury Lingerie"; the tempestuous, inspirational relationship with her husband and business partner; the disastrous impact of overexpansion and economic recession; litigious disputes over the use of her own name; and the ability, phoenix-like, to rebuild her business for a second time. All this in just thirty years.

It's a match: Janet Reger's complimentary lingerie looks include bras, panties, and briefs (*above*) in the same pretty motifs. Part floral, part see-through…these designs are blooming.

When a young student at the Leicester College of Technology presented a matching set of lingerie— bra, knickers and suspender belt—as her final year presentation, in 1953, her inspired idea gained immediate attention. It was a few years before Janet enjoyed commercial success with her idea, but in the meantime, the young designer took a variety of posts as a house designer for swimwear and underwear manufacturers, studying the disciplines and frustrations of mass manufacture.

Reger's ability was to coordinate cloth with cut, line with fit, and style with practicality and comfort. She looked for the underlying idea and then worked out how the garment should be cut and made. From the start she designed co-ordinated garments, a radical departure from the conventions of the time when underwear was black or white, except for salmon pink corsets.

When she met her future husband, Peter Reger, a young German, on a kibbutz in Israel in 1958, a professional relationship as well as a personal one was born. Peter Reger took on the role of selling and promoting Janet Reger's products, as well as marrying her within three years. They had a daughter, Aliza, and lived in Zurich, from where Reger worked as a freelance designer for a

number of European companies, before moving to London in 1965.

Once there, Peter took samples of Janet Reger's matching lingerie designs to show the buyers at Fenwicks and Selfridges, leading London department stores. With enthusiasm, they placed the first orders for Janet Reger's designs, which had caught the more liberated attitudes of the changing social climate of the 1960s. Women wanted to enjoy their underwear, and Janet Reger's innovative styles in pure silk caused a sensation. By 1967, Janet Reger Creations Ltd was established as a formal company, with a modest workshop, a production factory, and wholesale customers. Thanks to media interest, the name Reger quickly became synonymous with beautiful, youthful, sexy lingerie.

Next, Reger ventured into catalog selling. "The Bottom Drawer" was a hugely successful publication, offering a range of lingerie under her own label, with its distinctive trademark of the Dragonfly. This originated as a range of hand-painted designs on expensive silks, beautifully made, hand-finished and decorated with lace and appliqué—these were luxury items, and unique. Journalists, pop stars, and aristocrats from around the world visited the workshop—there was no shop—where Bianca Jagger, Angie Bowie, and

HRH Princess Anne were among the first customers. It was only a matter of time before a dedicated shop became a matter of necessity, to meet demand and interest.

Janet Reger boutiques soon opened in Beauchamp Place, Brook Street, and Bond Street in London, while in New York, Saks of Fifth Avenue placed its first orders. There too, clients included the rich and the famous, while for the first time men dared to buy lingerie for their wives and girlfriends.

Boom or bust?

A 1982 licensing deal with the lingerie manufacturer, Berlei was to prove disastrous for Janet Reger Creations Ltd, however. The company went into voluntary liquidation a year later, and Berlei purchased the "Janet Reger" trademark, although just three months later, Janet Reger reopened the doors in Beauchamp Place. Her loyal customers returned, spurning Berlei's Janet Reger range, and as Berlei's market flagged, it too went into receivership. Finally, after four years of litigation, Janet Reger was able to repurchase her own trademark, at a cost of £100,000 ($170 000). "In itself the trademark was a means to an end, but at the same time I had the sense to recognize that buying it would provide a solution that would eventually put an end to my financial miseries. I never doubted that if I could raise the money it would be possible to pay it back—and I have been proved right," said Janet Reger in her candid autobiography.

Her husband died in 1986, but Janet Reger continued to build her international business with her daughter Aliza. There

were licensing deals with the Janet Reger logo on bedlinen, window blinds, lampshades, slippers, hosiery, bathroom accessories such as tissue boxes and toilet bags, leisure wear, daywear, costume jewelry and precious jewels, swimwear, sunglasses, spectacles, handbags, and even a perfume, as well as non-couture underwear. From 1993 onwards, well known American stores such as Saks Fifth Avenue, Neiman Marcus, and Nordstrum, as well as a string of boutiques on Beverly Hills' famous Rodeo Drive, all stocked Janet Reger, whose appeal spread as far afield as Japan and even Dubai.

Hot stuff: A bustier and knickers (*above*) pack a punch in sizzly pink and black but Reger manages to soften the edges with ribbon and lace touches.

Frilly and fancy: Reger's lacy camisole and briefs (*below*) in soft, subtle, floaty colors with a delicate floral design add a feminine edge to under-dressing.

A Century of Lingerie
1900–2000

At the turn of the twentieth century women were

restrained in every sense, socially, financially, and

physically, by constricting, repressive underwear.

Through the subsequent years, women's lingerie

developed almost simultaneously with their

emancipation, reflecting the greater freedom and

independence that women gained as the century

progressed. At times this was accidental, a reaction

to events beyond women's control, such as global

war or financial depression, and at others, it was

self determined, as women's ideas about

themselves and their role in the world changed.

The shape of things past: this typical corset of the early
1900s (*top*) helped woman to achieve the classic hourglass
shape.
A push in the right direction: cleavage gets a boost with the
Ultra-bra (*right*), Gossard's revolutionary push-up.

It's a cinch: Marcel Rochas creates a new style of corsets in 1945 known as the "waspie" (*left*), nicknamed the "cincher" in the U.S.

Sheer delight: women all over the world are now wearing sheer tights (*right*) of all colors and styles.

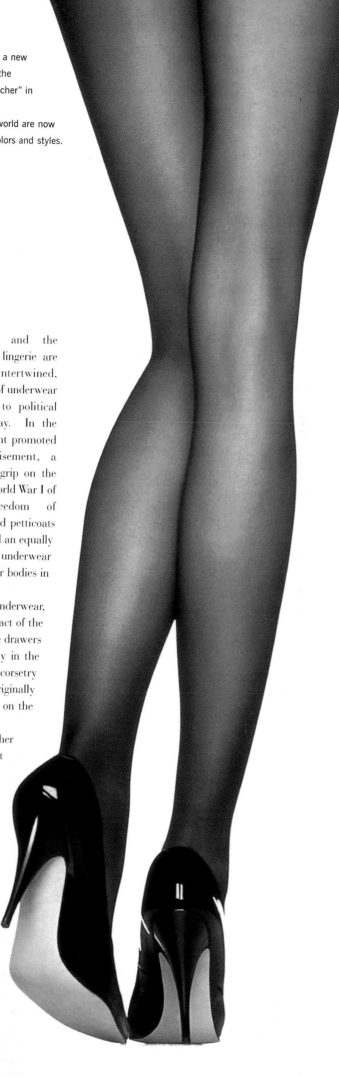

Female politics and the development of lingerie are remarkably intertwined, with new styles of underwear closely aligned to political issues of the day. In the 1910s the Suffragette Movement promoted emancipation and enfranchisement, a period when the corset's iron grip on the female form began to loosen. World War I of 1914–1918 demanded freedom of movement as women became involved in the war effort, and layers of impractical frilled petticoats were abandoned in favour of slimline uniforms. Some twenty years later, World War II had an equally profound effect, as rationing prohibited embellishment on lingerie and purely functional underwear emerged as a result. When the launch of the contraceptive Pill gave women control of their bodies in the 1960s, hemlines rose to tantalizing heights, and the girdle all but disappeared.

Women's increasing interest and participation in sport made new demands on their underwear, as did, inadvertently, the widespread growth of travel and transport of all types. The impact of the bicycle was immense, as it revealed the leg for the first time, and led to the modest, visible drawers (or bloomers), and tennis, golfing and horseriding, all popular pastimes for the wealthy in the 1910s, gave rise to the Sports Corset. In the 1930s, gymnasts appreciated the new, flexible corsetry which incorporated elastic, the forerunner of high performance fabrics such as Lycra. Originally introduced into active sportswear for athletics in the 1960s, Lycra had a radical impact on the figure-hugging bodies and panties of the 1980s.

It is impossible to underestimate the influence of the entertainment industry—whether music, film, or theatre—on lingerie styles. The dancing corset of the 1910s was a direct result of the tango craze, while jive music of the 1950s made full swinging petticoats essential for dancing the jitterbug. More recently, the 1978 disco-dance craze popularized dancewear, leading to the introduction of the body, and American actress and pop star Madonna made underwear, and particularly the push-up bra, her icon in the 1980s, taking it into the fashion mainstream. Cinema sirens of the 1930s, such as Marlene Dietrich and Greta Garbo, created the concept of sex appeal, which was epitomized by sexy lingerie. The studios were quick to exploit the idea, with "motion picture" departments in large clothes stores around the world, and Marilyn Monroe, Sophia Loren and Gina Lollabrigida, as well as Madonna, all influenced the design of lingerie in subsequent decades.

But the single most significant factor in lingerie's historical development has been fashion. As "foundationwear," underwear has always allowed women to create the fashionable shape of the day whatever their original body shape. Although the tightfitting bodices of the early 1900s have largely been abandoned in favour of more comfortable garments, the idea of restriction and reshaping is still with us one hundred years later.

A Golden Age

In 1901, years of industrial prosperity on both sides of the Atlantic ensured a social climate associated with stability, elegance, and grace, at least for the wealthy.

It was an exciting time, when the American inventor Henry Ford designed the first popular mass-produced automobile, the Model T, in 1908, and French pilot Blériot crossed the English Channel in an aeroplane for the first time.

A round of social engagements meant that clothes played an important role in the daily schedule of those in high society, and women were required to change their outfits as often as five times a day, their outer garments covering layers of underclothes beneath. Much underwear of the time was made from fine silks and lace, delicate fabrics which were easily damaged and required considerable laundering, starching, ironing, and mending. Most petticoats had sumptuously frilled edges—the swishing sound which they created was considered very sensual—and socialites spent up to a fifth of their annual dress allowance on underwear.

For most of the decade, both popular and high-society outer clothes were dominated by the fashionable S-bend silhouette. Its distinctive

1900

As well-bred women were allowed more physical freedom in the first years of the century, what they demanded from their clothes changed accordingly. Sports of all sorts became increasingly popular, especially cycling and tennis. Voluminous bloomers, named after their creator Mary Bloomer, were also known as "rational dress." They were worn under thin dresses for cycling, but were considered racy.

1903

Combinations, which combined two separate pieces of lingerie, such as a chemise and drawers, became increasingly popular in the early 1900s. Made of finest silk to maintain the slender silhouette of the day, many had frilly legs. A fine woolen version was introduced by Dr. Jaegar during this time to provide a healthy alternative for winter.

shape—with a large monobosom, tiny waist, and rounded behind—was created by the S-bend corset, a ferocious piece of underwear which distorted the spine and compressed the waist and abdomen. Although the look was generally matronly, one of the most popular characters of the time was the "Gibson Girl," a creation of the American illustrator Charles Dana Gibson. Between the 1890s and 1914, this youthful, independent, and active female character appeared in many magazines of the time, dressed in the ubiquitous S-bend corset but with outer clothes that laid the way for separates—long, tailored skirts and fitted blouses.

Beneath the tightly laced corset—from shoulder to thigh—would have been a chemise, while over the top were worn unseamed drawers with an open crotch which stretched to the knee, a camisole or corset cover, and as many as six layers of petticoats. Garters and stockings were attached to the corset, possibly with a jeweled clasp.

In 1907, French couturier Paul Poiret revolutionized both outer and underwear by introducing a more natural contour to clothes, releasing women from the tyranny of the corset. He was not the first to do so—Britain's well-known store Liberty had stocked "aesthetic dress" from the early 1900s, its loose, classical lines equally comfortable for women—but he was the first high-profile designer to abandon such artificial restrictions for women. It was the start of modern fashion.

19 OO's

1907

Parisian couturier Paul Poiret took the radical step of releasing women from their corsets, designing clothes for their natural shape. The Paris Chamber of Commerce was so alarmed by the possible repercussions of this move for the corset industry that they sent a delegation to Poiret to beg him to change his mind. He refused.

1909

Night-time wear was as varied as daytime clothes, with workaday flannelette nightgowns for cold winter nights, gowns of fine lawn trimmed with lace for romantic encounters, and even pajamas. Pajamas were first worn by men in England in the seventeenth century, their design drawn from similar Indian and Persian garments—*pae*, meaning foot, or leg, and *jamah*, meaning clothing or garment, both from ancient Persian. Girls and women started to wear pajamas in the early twentieth century, accompanied by *negligées* and *peignoirs*.

1906

Modesty vests—a small square of lawn, lace, or silk pinned to the underside of the neckline—became widely worn as the long tailored skirts and fitted blouses popularized by the Gibson Girl made their appearance. For some women, used to the high collars of earlier dress, the open neck of a shirt was simply too revealing, not to mention unhealthy.

New Attitudes for a New Era

On both sides of the Atlantic, there was an atmosphere of peace, prosperity, and optimism in 1910. When women rejected the restrictions of their corsets in 1915, it gave them a symbolic as well as a physical freedom.

The suffragette movement, led by women in search of independent recognition and the right to vote through organized protest, was gaining momentum.

The arrival of Serge Diaghilev's Ballet Russe in Paris in 1909 had an international visual, cultural, and aesthetic impact throughout Europe, and then further afield. Lev Bakst's designs for the dancers used rich fabrics and exotic colors; and turbaned headdresses and sumptuous colors, from golden yellow, ruby, and scarlet to turquoise, purple, jade green, and black, soon appeared in the wardrobes of the fashionable.

Beneath the floor-length dresses, the precursors to today's underwear were making their first appearance. The brassière came into use from around 1913, although who exactly invented it is a matter of debate, and by 1916, the British magazine *The Lady* was commenting,

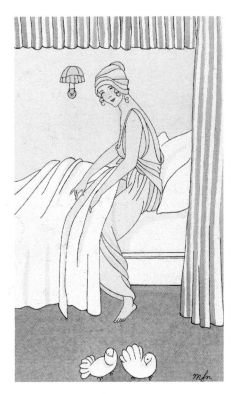

1911

Luxurious pajamas of brightly colored silk and satin appeared in the bedroom, worn with turbans and "coats" of equally fine fabrics. They were inspired by Serge Diaghilev's Ballet Russe, who arrived in Europe in 1909 to huge acclaim, dressed in the exotic designs of Lev Bakst.

1912

Stockings made from an early form of rayon, known before 1926 as artificial silk, were manufactured by the American firm Viscose Company Stockings. For the first time ever, women of all social backgrounds were able to enjoy the luxury of fitted stockings, a necessity once skirt lengths rose in the middle of the decade.

1913

A new type of woven elasticized material emerged in the United States, and was incorporated into the American slip-on, a supportive garment worn by those who had abandoned the whalebone corset during the tango dance craze of the 1910s.

"French and American women all wear them and so must we." Combinations were often worn with the brassière, many beautifully made in silk and fine cotton and carefully trimmed and embroidered.

One of the major factors in the decline of the corset was the tango dance craze which swept through the Americas and Europe. As dancing to ragtime was vitually impossible in tightly boned and laced corsets—the sensational American dancer Josephine Baker proved this with her free and athletic dance style—the "dancing corset" was invented.

But World War I sounded the death knell for old-fashioned corsets. Women involved in the war effort, many working for the first time as drivers, bus conductors, and in factories, rejected both corsets and full petticoats as impractical. By the end of the decade, women were wearing shorter, loose-waisted dresses with fewer layers of underwear.

In the years following the war's end in 1918, they never reverted to the contradictory constraints of corsets and excesses of petticoats experienced during the belle époque directly preceding WWI, despite many invitations to do so.

19 10's

1914

Just before a dance, a young American debutante Mary Phelps Jacob and her maid invented their brassière, made from two handkerchiefs and a piece of ribbon. The boneless, midriff-free bra was revolutionary, flattening the bust and pushing it downward into the classic "flapper" shape.

1914

The outbreak of World War I sounded the death knell for the corset as women required far more physical freedom to carry out their war work. Metal-boned corsets were banned from munitions factories.

1916

Women working began to have an impact on fashion and style, as full-length dresses were clearly impractical for those in physical occupations, such as nurses. Skirt lengths rose to mid-calf, a move which was quickly followed by the creation of short drawers—the forerunner to today's panties. These had a garter at mid-thigh, to which the newly fashionable stockings were attached.

The Roaring Twenties

At the dawn of the 1920s, all were determined to forget the privations of the war years, and the 1920s became an era of excesses. The younger social set, who soon became known as "bright young things," dressed in a way that was deliberately decadent, exciting, and provocative.

Cropped hair, kohl-rimmed eyes and short skirts were a radical expression of the beliefs of the young social set of the 1920s, and symbolized a hard-won freedom. Liberated women could be seen smoking (using long cigarette holders as essential fashion accessories), eating in public without chaperones, and drinking exotic cocktails.

The era was a melting pot of multicultural ideas and influences, both visually and socially. On both sides of the Atlantic, people flocked to the clubs to hear the sounds of jazz artists such as Duke Ellington, although in the United States, those who wanted to drink were driven underground by the Prohibition Laws, which forbade the production and sale of liquor. At the famous Cotton Club in Harlem, mobsters mixed with the cream of American society, while in Paris the artists Jean Cocteau and Pablo Picasso worked alongside the designer Coco Chanel and choreographer Serge Diaghilev to produce the ballet *Le Train Bleu*. The discovery of Tutankhamen's tomb also led to a passion for anything Egyptian.

1922

The term "lingerie" appears for the first time, replacing the more mundane "corsetry" previously used. This reflected the vogue for indulgent and feminine underwear that was worn underneath the unfussy, streamlined flapper dresses. *Crêpe de chine*, pleated chiffon, silk tricot, and heavy crêpe satins all found their way into luxurious undergarments.

1921

French tennis champion Susanne Lenglen epitomized the 1920s New Woman, dressed from head to toe in clothes by French couturier Jean Patou. Her androgynous look, see Louise Brooks (*above*), was a sign of the times, with the leg, and its enclosing stocking, the center of attention—not to mention the strip of bare thigh that showed itself between the top of her stockings and short dress hem.

1924

During the twenties, Coco Chanel first presented her collections of women's wear made of unromantic jersey cotton, her efforts were ridiculed. But before long, the elegance and comfort of Chanel's clothes soon convinced even the most sceptical, who wore them over a variety of cami-knickers and wide-legged French knickers.

All areas of design were influenced by the *Exposition des Arts Décoratifs et Industriels Modernes*, held in Paris in 1925. Glamor was in, and it could be bought with recently acquired riches as social mobility took hold in earnest. As the leg was revealed for the first time in fashion's history, geometric Art Deco patterns were seen everywhere, from stockings to skyscrapers.

Flat chest and long, lean body was the ideal—a precocious look known as the *Garçonne* style in France—and women bound their breasts and dieted to extremes to achieve it. But despite the boyishness of the "flappers," women wore indulgent and ultimately feminine garments under the streamlined, androgynous outerwear.

Sexual mores underwent a revolution, spurred on by the sexy sirens of Hollywood. Rudolph Valentino was a massive heart throb,

causing a sensation by his performance in *The Sheik* (1921). His many female admirers, enraptured, even sent him their lingerie with their fan mail. But even Hollywood could not keep reality at bay. When the American Stock Exchange collapsed in 1929, plunging the United States into crisis and the Depression of the 1930s, the financial shock waves were felt around the world.

19'20's

1925

Although the first brassières had simply flattened the breasts in line with the fashion of the time, the Kestos bra was the first commerical success as a shaped brassière. Its elastic backing, darts under the bust, and button fastening soon made it the first choice for women searching for a supportive undergarment.

1926

By the time the *Garçonne*, or flapper, look reached its peak, with hemlines above the knee for the first time, never had so much leg been seen. Silk stockings, often wildly decorated with patterns and motifs, were worn rolled above the knee and held up with garters. Early forms of rayon provided a more downmarket version for the less wealthy, bought for a quarter of the price of silk stockings, although they developed runs far more easily.

1927

As hemlines rose, so the stately Princess petticoat became redundant after forty years of use. It too was shortened, becoming known first as the Princess slip and then simply as a slip.

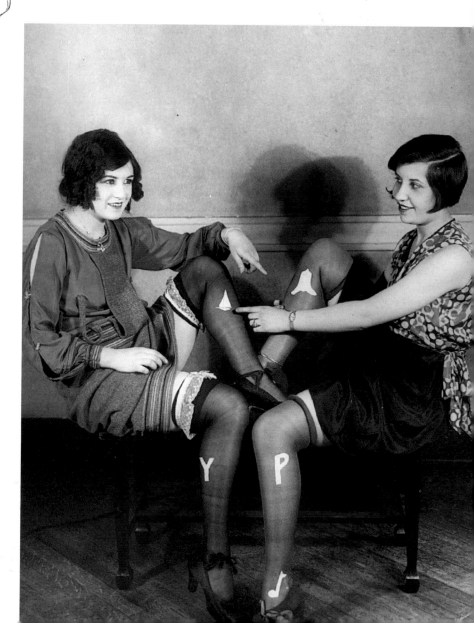

Seriously Thirty Somethings

The escapism that Hollywood offered from the dire reality of the Depression years led to weekly audiences for the latest movies of over 85 million in America, with similarly large numbers in Europe, riveted as they were by the new generation of sex sirens, such as Marlene Dietrich, Jean Harlow, and Mae West.

In Europe and America large numbers of men and women were drawn to the cinema, and movie moguls were quick to recognize the marketing potential of the situation. They sold the style, clothes, and cosmetics of the stars through vehicles such as film magazines, which advised women how to achieve the look they craved.

Slinky fabrics such as satin and *crêpe de chine*, which clung to the body, were used to create the sinuous lines of the day, designed both for the Hollywood stars and for the richest haute couture clients by American and French designers such as Adrian and Madame Grès (who worked under the name Alix). The bias cut—where the fabric was cut across its natural grain—typified the time, introduced by French couturier Madeleine Vionnet and used to great effect. The long silhouette that bias cutting created flowed over hips and waist, and separated the breasts. The bust was back in vogue.

A new style of lingerie was essential to complement this svelte, sensuous figure, and much of it, particularly corsetry, incorporated the new man-made fibers, from rayon to elasticized net. Such items were practical but often dull, as ornamentation was kept to a minimum to maintain the smooth line. "Too much practical lingerie makes a dull

1931

Paris fashions were dominated by the designs of Adrian, Madame Grès (who designed under the name Alix), and Madame Vionnet. The long, sensuous dress lines created by cutting fashionable slinky fabrics such as satin and *crêpe de chine* on the bias brought the bust back into vogue. As a result, the bra, as it was by now commonly called, was often made with cups for added "uplift," a popular term at the time. Many of the Paris dresses were backless, leading to the introduction of the first strapless bra in 1934.

1932

Slim yoked panties were commonly worn under the draped dresses of the day, chosen to maintain the smooth hip line. Heavier women often wore a lightweight corset over the panties for added control, and by 1935 many of these were closed with a zipper (zip).

1934

As in the prevous decade, the stars of Hollywood had an enormous effect on women's fashions. Copies of the stars' costumes could be bought in the "cinema department" of large clothes stores. In one film starring Clark Gable, *It Happened One Night*, the French-born actress Claudette Colbert stripped down to her underwear, provoking a flurry of copycat fashions.

woman. An occasional frill is good for the soul," advised British *Vogue*, and those who agreed turned to romantic underwear that looked back to the first years of the century.

In 1939, a completely new style was shown at the Paris Spring collections, the new hourglass figure featuring a nipped-in waist and accentuated hips and bosom. But events were to overtake this new direction in fashion, as in the same year, the world was plunged back into crisis with the outbreak of World War II. It would be almost a decade before such fashions would be seen again.

19 30's

1935

"You can't have any bulges in your figure!" declared British *Vogue*, and women flocked to buy the new corselettes that included elasticized panels. Among the most popular were Sleekies, an all-in-one that included a bra and garters.

1935

Warner introduced bras with cup fittings for the first time, realizing that the measurement of the bust and the size of the breasts were two different things.

1937

Toward the end of the decade, American manufacturers DuPont patented the first nylon. Light, strong, and supple, nylon could be knitted by machine into various weights (or deniers) and required no ironing—it simply dripped dry. It was the ideal material for bras and was soon found in all types of undergarments, despite the outbreak of World War II.

129

Make Do and Mend

The impact of the outbreak of World War II was immeasurable. Almost overnight, glamor disappeared in Europe as austerity and rationing took hold, to be replaced by Utility Clothing and women in military uniform. Similar restrictions took place in America, but they were minimal compared to Europe.

The United States did not experience extreme wartime rationing and restrictions until the War Production Board imposed guidelines in 1943, but even these were minimal compared to the restrictions experienced in Britain.

Cut off from Europe until 1944, American industries of all sorts, including lingerie, took a new direction. They were more protected from the war than similar European firms, and wealthier, too. American designers developed a range of new manufacturing techniques and materials, helped in some cases by designers driven out of Europe by Fascism, and in the field of lingerie, outstripped European competitors for the first time.

Hollywood's influence continued to grow, and during the war years a stream of morale-boosting films flooded the world, such as *The Fleet's In* (1942) and *Tin Pan Alley* (1943.) The actress Betty Grable became the pin-up of servicemen of all nationalities.

In Europe, materials were in scarce supply, and only essential fabrics were readily available. All clothes, including lingerie, were designed to be practical and durable as "Make Do and Mend" became the British Board of Trade's slogan. The tight waist of uniforms promoted the

1941

American underwear manufacturers took the lead over their European competitors as rationing hit home in Europe. Among the new fabrics they developed was Elastex. In Europe, American GIs impressed women with gifts of nylon stockings, as silk and rayon stockings were only available on the black market.

1942

In Britain, the Board of Trade introduced its Utility Scheme, which banned all trimmings such as lace and embroidery on any type of clothing. Black and white replaced the pinks of earlier lingerie, and most undergarments were mass produced, and often stamped with the CC41 label. Many underwear factories were turned over to the production of parachutes and similar items.

1943

During the war years, tightly-belted uniforms drew attention to the waistline. Fewer women wore a full corset, however, preferring the more modern girdle under skirts or cutaway panties under trousers. Some of these brief knickers included elsticized side panels for control.

hourglass silhouette, with the bust emphasized and shorter hemlines that fell just above the knee, which inevitably drew attention to the legs. Where stockings were in short supply, some women resorted to dyeing their legs with liquid makeup or coffee, and drawing a seam line down the back with an eyebrow pencil.

By the time World War II was over, in 1945, the United States was undisputably the most powerful, and the richest, nation in the world, whose movie business ensured that its influence was felt all around the globe. Fabric restrictions were lifted in the U.S. in 1946, but not until 1949 in Europe. For the first time, American clothes designers such as Claire McCardell were taken seriously in Europe, while the commercial potential of the American market was not lost on European designers.

When Christian Dior launched his extravagant New Look in February 1947, few European women would have been able to afford the 25 yards (30 m) of material the full skirts required. Nonetheless, the desire to leave behind the practicality and austerity of the war years won out, and women strove to imitate the look, which demanded a radical change in lingerie to create the tiny waist and full skirts.

19 40's

1947

Christian Dior unveiled his New Look collection. Its tiny, cinched waist and full skirts over padded hips and petticoats reveled in excess after the restrictions of the war years. Not everyone was impressed, though. *The Picture Post* commented "There can be no question about the entire unsuitability of these new fashions for our present life and times…"

1945

Marcel Rochas first manufactured the waspie, a new style of corset know as the cincher in the U.S. and the *guimpe* or *corset guêpière* in France. Its tiny, boned waistband of 5–8 inches (13–20 cm) hooked at the back to give even the thinnest women a contour.

1948

The famous lingerie manufacturer Frederick's of Hollywood introduced the Rising Star, the world's first push-up bra. This signaled the return of the bust being fashionable after years of focusing on the waist.

Riding the Waves of Affluence

The 1950s began on both sides of the Atlantic on an optimistic note. It was a time for reconciliation and adjusting to a settled peacetime economy in which the world could build its future as the technological advancements developed during World War II were applied to all aspects of manufacturing.

The industrial economy of the U.S. led to a large and affluent workforce whose children were developing minds of their own. By the early 1950s, teenagers were jiving to the tunes of Elvis Presley and other artists and within a few years, rock'n'roll had swept the world, its addicts dressed in full skirts and net petticoats that had their origins in Dior's New Look.

The tight waist of Dior's New Look was achieved by wearing girdles extended over the waist, almost to the bra line, as well as all-in-one corselettes to control midriff bulge. From the early 1950s, several couture houses launched their own "foundationwear" lines—"corsetry" was considered vulgar—a move matched by lingerie manufacturers for the mass market, who began to launch their own brand names to build customer loyalty.

1950

Overtly sexy and provocative, Dior's New Look was much admired by women, who opted for the sharply defined breasts, narrow torso, sloping hips, and long legs that the style produced. Although still slender, the waist was less extreme than in the '40s, often controlled by an all-in-one corselette.

1955

Couturiers such as Christian Dior launched their own lingerie, or "foundationwear," labels to be worn under their creations. The merging of outer and underwear could be seen in the torsolette, a luxury version of the corset that was backless, strapless, and décolleté. In some cases, it was beaded and embroidered, and worn over an evening skirt.

1954

The American firm Silhouette was the first to incorporate two-way stretch fabric into a corset, the "Little X." These elastic-based corsets could manipulate the figure into a variety of sexy shapes.

Another branch of the entertainment industry was equally influential on the young, and not so young. Rebellious attitudes were captured on screen in films such as *On the Waterfront* and *Rebel Without a Cause*, while Marilyn Monroe, Jane Mansfield, Diana Dors, Sophia Loren, Elizabeth Taylor, and Brigitte Bardot presented the look of the day. "Sweater Girl" Lana Turner was particularly admired by both sexes, her tight-fitting sweaters worn over bras reinforced with stiffening points, although it was the actress Jane Russell's "Cantilever" bra which drew the most attention, when she wore it in the film *The Outlaws* in 1957 when it was finally released.

There were more changes to come as the 1960s arrived. The teenage revolution had started, taking its lead from Hollywood actors and actresses once again, while the marriage of actress Grace Kelly to Prince Rainier of Monaco underlined how glamorous, self-made Hollywood beauties were seen as equals to the aristocracy. The more casual lifestyle on the horizon would bring more casual clothes and the lingerie to accompany them.

19**50's**

1956

Hollywood continued to exert its influence on everyday fashions and styles. Sultry stars such as Carol Baker in *Baby Doll* lounged across the silver screens in layered, ruched, and beribboned nighties made from the new textiles, including drip-dry nylon. The film was denied a Production Code Administration Seal of Approval and was condemned by the Legion of Decency.

1957

The most infamous bra of the decade was the Cantilever bra, designed by aeronautical engineer Howard Hughes. The actress, Jane Russell, wore the bra in the film, *The Outlaws*. Its unique design was based on the principal of a suspension bridge, and its impressive dimensions led to a spate of falsies to ensure the same voluptuous look for everyone.

1959

When Fibre K, later to be known as Lycra, was launched, the lingerie industry was quick to see its potential, incorporating the fabric into the entire spectrum of underwear. As often as not, it was combined with the new dyeing techniques that allowed intense colors and printed patterns to be applied to even the cheapest garments.

Street Scene

The 1960s was a decade of great contrasts. On the one hand, teenagers revolted against the order of the establishment in an unprecedented manner on both sides of the Atlantic, and on the other, a deep-seated, underlying conservatism showed its face in a return to classic dress styles.

The 1960s was a decade of great contrasts. On the one hand, teenagers revolted against the order of the Establishment in an unprecedented manner on both sides of the Atlantic, creating their own dress code, music, and a fiercely independent attitude. And on the other, a deep-seated, underlying conservatism showed its face in a return to classic dress styles as the Paris couturiers regained their status.

For the first time, young women dressed differently from their mothers and established their own style for clothes and accessories as the fashion boutique sprang up, catering exclusively for a young clientele. Much of the prevailing style was set in London, where the designer Mary Quant and her partner Alistair Plunkett-Green had opened the first boutique—Bazaar—on the King's Road in 1955. Her colorful, playful clothes were a huge success with young women; her miniskirts worn with the brightly colored and textured tights also

1960

During the age of the teens, followers of fashion rejected the curves of the 1950s and turned to the tall, thin, willowy frame that epitomized the decade. The boned corset was no longer required as fashions, attitudes, and new elasticized fabrics such as Lycra made it redundant.

1963

The British designer Mary Quant launched her Ginger Group collection of sweaters, dresses, and skirts. Their short hemlines, which became shorter as the decade progressed, rendered stockings impractical and led to the widespread use of pantyhose.

1963

The launch of the contraceptive pill revolutionized women's attitudes to their sexuality. The bottom became a focus in design, just one of a number of erogenous zones—the thigh, the midriff— that were publicly displayed. Under tight jeans, minimal underwear was required.

designed by Quant became a feature of the decade. Quant's second store opened in fashionable Knightsbridge in 1963, the same year that another London designer, Polish-born Barbara Hulanicki, opened the equally influential clothes store Biba.

In 1963, the contraceptive pill was launched, liberating women from the burden of pregnancy on a big scale for the first time. Almost simultaneously, fashion honed in on the bottom as an erogenous zone, and shapes in lingerie changed radically. By the end of the 1960s, jeans were the uniform of the young, worn over bikini briefs.

In 1965, the British pop groups The Beatles and later The Rolling Stones took their music to the U.S., where girls followed the British example, screaming at pop concerts and mobbing their idols. But while such anarchy hit the headlines, running in parallel was a more conservative mood. A new style of restrained glamor, captured by the American president's wife Jackie Kennedy at The White House, could

be found both in the United States and Europe, where the French actress Catherine Deneuve was dressed by Yves St Laurent and Audrey Hepburn, the English star of *Breakfast at Tiffany's* (1961), was dressed by Givenchy. For the wealthy at least, the focus had returned to the couturiers of Paris.

19 60's

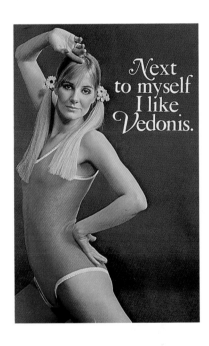

1966

Although younger women wore less and less underwear, those over the age of 30 still clung to stockings, suspenders, and supportive panty girdles. As a concession to the times, however, many of these employed a far bolder use of color and pattern than earlier examples, such as those produced by Kayser Bond.

1967

The new nylon fabrics and bright colors were used in short, frilly nightgowns and teddies in powder blue, blush pink, or floral patterns. Similarly, Lycra found its way into all manner of swimwear which so closey resembled underwear than many young women wore it for both.

1964

As the padded, shaped bra was rejected by women struggling to redefine their femininity, Rudi Gernreich launched his "no-bra bra" in response. His aim was to design a bra that covered the breasts comfortably without molding them into specific shapes.

1968

As the 1960s drew to a close, science fiction developed a cult following with films such as *Barbarella*. In it, actress Jane Fonda appeared shackled in fetishistic corsets, a sign of times to come.

Back to Nature

The rebelliousness of the 1960s matured into a new awareness in the 1970s—an understanding that individuality in fashion was just as important as the guidelines laid down by style magazines.

Myriad influences dominated the fashions of the early decade, from a continuing interest in peasant dress and culture around the world—started by the 1960 hippy movement—to a new social conscience, an awareness for the environment, and a desire for a sympathetic natural look. In Britain, designers such as Zandra Rhodes and Laura Ashley created full flowing robes in floating fabrics, but in both the U.S. and Europe, denim was the unwritten uniform of the young.

Jeans with wide flared legs were worn with voile and natural cotton shirts over as little underwear as possible. The desire for a "natural look" appeared in lingerie as well as on stage with such productions as *Hair* as nudity became all the rage. Despite the fact that the bra was briefly regarded with disdain by the militant wing of the growing Women's Movement as a symbol of female repression, it never

1972
The halterneck bra arrived, one of a variety of bra shapes and styles that appeared in the fashionable fabrics of the day.

1971
American manufacturers DuPont created Spandex, or satin-stitch, which was renamed Elastane in 1976. Its smooth finish made it ideal for controlling and shaping larger bodies, and it was extensively used in girdles.

1973
Matching sets of lingerie are causing a stir—bras, panties, and garter belts are produced by the designer Janet Reger in lace and satin. Intimate, exciting, and sensual, the sets fulfilled a new desire for romance that was evident in the 1970s.

completely faded away. Some women picketed the flagship store of Frederick's of Hollywood, established by American lingerie designer Frederick Mellinger, who responded by remarking that "the law of gravity will win out." In the ensuing publicity, bra sales soared.

The 1970s saw a number of technical innovations and fabric developments which the lingerie industry was quick to adopt. Traditional corsetry was outdated, and totally rejected by a generation who were increasingly body, diet, exercise, and health conscious. As the aerobics and personal fitness craze took hold, dancewear such as leotards and tights crossed over into both under and outerwear and were seen everywhere. Casual wear had truly arrived, bringing with it a more casual approach to life in general.

By the end of the decade, cleavage was making a comeback. New formed bras gave a seamfree, perfectly fitting shape which banished the visible lines under the figure-hugging clothes of the day and heralded the T-shirt bra and crop tops of the following years. This was the salvation the lingerie industry had hoped for.

19**70's**

1979

The release of the film *Grease*, starring John Travolta and Olivia Newton-John, spawned a dance and fitness craze that continued to grow through the following decade. Sleek, Lycra-based catsuits and leotards left nothing to the imagination, and were soon worn both in and out of dance studios.

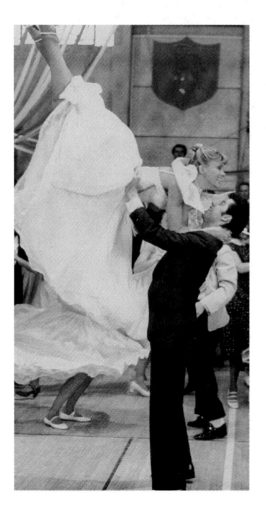

1974

With the anarchic punk movement well underway in Britain, pop promoter Malcolm McClaren signed a leading punk band, the Sex Pistols. His partner, designer Vivienne Westwood, created the band's image, with laddered fishnet stockings, bras worn as outerwear, and overt references to bondage practices.

Designer Labels

As an era when money talked, the 1980s were marked by the importance of image. Designer label clothes from Katherine Hamnett to Georgio Armani adorned the bodies of gym-honed women, many of whom drove fast cars from Porsches to Turbo Saabs.

Women's financial independence, based on increasing opportunity in the workplace, was expressed by "power dressing," seen in its extremes on television series such as *Dallas*. As often as not, the professional woman wore an elegant miniskirt with high-heeled shoes and severely tailored, padded shouldered jackets. Beneath the business suit, however, women retained their silky camisoles and lacy bras, supplied by such mail-order firms as Victoria's Secret and lingerie designers, such as Frenchwoman Chantal Thomass, and Pascale Madonna.

As the fitness craze continued, the well-cut and contoured bra and body was on offer for the first time, evolved from sportswear worn in health clubs. There was a spate of unisex underwear, featuring a wide elastic waistband similar to that found on men's underwear, but by the mid 1980s women were demanding a softer styling in reaction to the severity of the prevalent underwear. Sensuality returned, and basques were revived for evening dress with matching briefs and stockings.

Awareness of western fashion design grew in the Far East, thanks to a number of talented Japanese designers working in Europe, including

1982

Debbie Moore, founder of the hugely successful Pineapple dance and fitness studios, based in London, floated the company on the stock market. Her success stemmed largely from her collection of sporty bodywear made from stretch Lycra, which was sold under the Pineapple brand name.

1983

A number of designers picked up on the punk ideas of the 1970s, including Jean Paul Gaultier, Thierry Mugler, and John Galliano. They went on to create entire collections around bras, corsets, and basques.

Rei Kuwakubo, founder of the fashion house Comme des Garçons. The lingerie industry began to target markets in the East, building on the popularity of designers such as Vivienne Westwood.

The first contemporary designer to promote underwear as outerwear, Westwood was hugely influential on other young and talented designers, including John Galliano, Thierry Mugler, and Jean-Paul Gaultier. Inspired by Westwood as well as the 1970s punk street fashions of which she was a part, a number of collections appeared at the Paris couture shows where corsetry was employed as fashionable outerwear. Such exposure ensured that the corset was to make a comeback in the 1990s.

19 80's

1984

Unisex underwear such as printed boxer shorts, underskirts (singlets), and panties with outer seams made an appearance, similar in color, shape, and fabric to some of the sportswear already on sale. In many cases, these carried the name of a known designer, such as Calvin Klein, as couture houses expanded into more downmarket lines such as tights, stockings, and underwear.

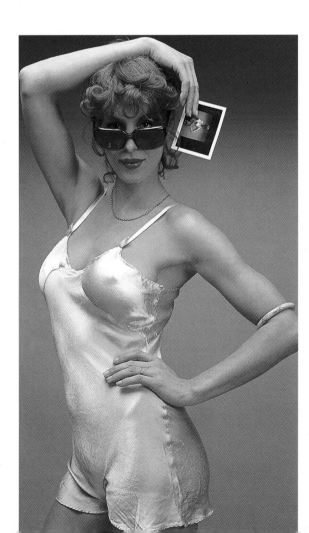

1985

The teddy made a comeback, replacing the cami-knicker as women yearned for less puritanical underwear. Stockings returned, as did frills, pleats, and lace.

1987

Vivienne Westwood astonished fashion commentators with her Statue of Liberty corset, which compressed the breast and thrust the bosom up and forward. Thereafter, the corset played an essential part of all her designs, as seen above, and was extremely influential on street and couture fashions alike.

139

Back to the Future

The center of attention in the lingerie world during the 1990s was the bust. A fashion dichotomy emerged, in which it was necessary to have both a flat chest and a fulsome bosom to achieve "the look" of the day.

Throughout the 1990s, the brash materialism of the 1980s began to subside, with a growing awareness of ecological concerns and a new realism on both sides of the Atlantic about the high cost to all of the luxurious Western lifestyle. Women, and especially young women, were relaxed enough in their new freedoms, both sexual and professional, to dress in a "look-but-don't-touch" fashion that proclaimed their self-assertive sexuality.

On the catwalk, the supermodel figure for the 1990s was epitomized by the waiflike forms of Kate Moss and Naomi Campbell. Such very thin bodies had little need for an uplifting bra. Fashion designers such as Gianni Versace, John Rochas, and Antonio Berardi promoted transparent chiffon shirts and skirts which could be worn by these relatively flat-chested models without underwear, giving the see-through look a 1990s twist. But for the more modest, and for those to whom nature had been generous, lingerie manufacturers such as Gossard and Calvin Klein responded with a new generation of "second skin" garments in flesh colors, designed to disguise and reveal the breast simultaneously.

1990

Pop star and actress Madonna embarked on her infamous "Blonde Ambition" world tour, dressed by Jean-Paul Gaultier in a sculptured corset with conical breasts. The stitching on the cones was reminiscent of 1950s bras.

1992

The Ultrabra from Gossard reinvented the cleavage, lifting the bosom so it swelled over the cup. It was not long before Playtex entered the market with its own version, the Wonderbra, starting the most competitive, and possibly most popular, advertising campaign ever known for lingerie, now known as the Bra Wars.

1994

Joseph Corré, son of Vivienne Westwood and Malcolm McClaren, opened a specialist lingerie shop in London, Agent Provocateur, with his partner Serena Rees. Their vast collection of lingerie celebrates the fact that women have a right to be proud of their body, whatever its shape and size, as they sell to women "who are in control of their lives."

Designers Vivienne Westwood, Jean-Paul Gaultier, Alexander McQueen, and Christian Lacroix all used the traditional corset as a source of inspiration for their haute couture designs. Their outfits employed the corsets as outerwear, rather than lingerie, a trend that was also seen in a vogue for slip dresses. Made of satin and lace, these marked the return of the petticoat, but as with the corset, were no longer to be hidden under layers of more modest clothing.

Within one hundred years, the fabrics, purpose, and shape of lingerie had evolved almost beyond recognition. The functional, restrained, and restraining foundationwear of the 1900s—a woman's most intimate garments—were on display as a matter of course by the year 2000. Few could have envisaged such a dramatic change in moral and personal values. Few could have imagined the impact of Lycra.

1990's

1991

The 1990s dance scene brought lingerie into the limelight. Shiny satin bras and cycling shorts were the thing to wear when clubbing or raving. Lingerie appeared in a spectrum of strong colors, including maroon, brown, purple, and bottle green, as did the crop tops, derived from sports and dancewear, designed to reveal pierced navels and other body parts.

1996

Contemporary tights such as the Secret Slimmer from Pretty Polly incorporate a modern girdlelike panel into the tight panties to create the perfect silhouette, remodeling and shaping the hips, thighs, and bottom, and slimming the waist. Oroblu introduced tights to sculpture the body and even banish cellulite, and stockings made a comeback, worn with the latest corsets.

1997

Victoria's Secret, a mail order business that specializes in indulgent and romantic underwear, has annual sales of over $3 billion, as women worldwide opt for its luxurious bras, panties, camisoles, sleepwear, and accessories.

CREDITS

Quarto would like to acknowledge and thank the following sources for permission to reproduce images on the following pages.

Agent Provocateur: 55, 65 br, 90 tl, 102 bl; Annie's, London: 34 bl; Berlei Archives; 15 br, 51 t, 106, 129; Bjorn Borg: 78 tl & bl; Le Bourget: 50 bl; Corbis-Bettmann UPI: 14 b, 16 br, 18, 23 b, 42, 45 br, 46 b, 60 l, 61 r & l, 62 br, 70, 72, 73, 75 bl, 76 br, 77 t, 79 b, 84, 86 b, 96, 98 t & b, 99 t & b, 100 b, 113 t r, 114 l, 120 l & r, 121 l & r, 122 l & c, 123 c, r & l, 124 r & l, 125, 128 l, 135 r & l, 136 r, 138 l; Damart: 39; Dolce & Gabbana: 22 l, 92; Frederick's of Hollywood 21 tr, 47 tl, 94, 95; Jean

Paul Gaultier: 54; Gossard (Jean Bennett Publicity): 43, 51b, 52-53, 91 l, 138 c; Hanro: 38; Hulton Getty: 31 b r, 35 t, 74 tl, 132 bl, 133 r; Imperial War Museum (photo courtesy of Princess Galitzine); Jerry Mason, London, England: 35 br; 47 tr & br, 75 t, 89 tl, 137 l; Alec Keeper 23 t; Marks and Spencer Archives: 29, 33 bl, bc, br, 68, 69; Flora Nikrooz: 93, La Perla: 49 r, 50 r, 63 br, 66; Pineapple: 76 l, 82, 83, 136 l, 138 r; Pretty Polly: 97, 107, 139 r; Mary Quant: 36 cl, 37 l, 65 tl, 85, 104, 105; Janet Reger: 37 r, 118, 119; Rigby and Peller: 26, 91 r; Silhouette: 134 l; Sloggi: 57, 67, 76 tr; Tony Stone: 115; Chantal Thomas 40, 41; Triumph: 50 tl; Victoria's Secret: 77 b, 116, 117; Wacoal: 25, 26; Warners: 45 tl; Vivienne Westwood: 137 r; Wolford: 80, 81.

Whilst every effort has been made to contact all copyright holders we apologise for any omissions.
All other photographs are the copyright of Quarto Publishing plc.

Quarto would also particularly like to thank Angela Messala, Gossard; the Berlei archive; Trudy Wilson, archive, picture research and photography; Philip Warren, Wygston Costume Museum, Leicestershire; Mark Haley, contour support specialist, Siemon Scamell-Katz, enhancements; Emily Slocock, photography, Rachel Toner, Warners (UK) International; the lingerie department of Fenwick of Bond Street; Loren Auerbach; and Lyndsay Russell.